. . .THE REQUEST
TO RENAME THE CITY OF PETROGRAD AFTER LENIN,
PUT FORWARD BY THE PETROGRAD SOVIET OF WORKERS',
PEASANTS' AND RED ARMY SOLDIERS' DEPUTIES
AND SUPPORTED BY THE WORKERS
OF ALL PETROGRAD PLANTS AND FACTORIES,
IS HEREBY GRANTED.
LET THIS LARGEST CENTRE OF PROLETARIAN REVOLUTION
BE HEREAFTER FOREVER LINKED WITH THE NAME
OF THE GREATEST LEADER OF THE PROLETARIAT —
VLADIMIR ILYICH ULYANOV (LENIN).

RESOLUTION OF THE SECOND CONGRESS OF SOVIETS
OF THE USSR. JANUARY 26, 1924

Panorama of the central part of Leningrad

LENINGRAD

Art & Architecture

Aurora Art Publishers
Leningrad

Introduced by Lev Uspensky

Compiled and designed by Gennady Gubanov
and Leonid Zykov

Translated from the Russian by William Freeman,
Yury Nemetsky and Bella Vlader

© Aurora Art Publishers, Leningrad, 1985, 1990
Printed and bound in Austria by Globus, Vienna

Л $\frac{4902020000\text{-}879}{023(01)\text{-}90}$ без объявления

ISBN 5-7300-0437-0

Some cities live quietly and peacefully for many centuries. Year after year they remain far removed from the tumultuous flow of historical events. Generations come and go, the years pass by, but nothing important, nothing truly earth-shaking ever happens. These cities intrude on no one, and no one intrudes on them. It is as if they hardly existed at all.

But there are cities of quite another kind. From the very first they seethe and boil without stopping. Their travails are heard around the world. They change with every passing year, and the changes remain indelibly etched on the fate of mankind. Rome was once such a city, Paris is now such a city, and Moscow, the capital and very heart of our country, is such a city. And, history tells us, Leningrad is one of these cities.

This city, "gem of the Northern world", has stood on the banks of the Neva for almost 300 years. This is not a very long time; there still are people living who are one-third as old as Leningrad. But what an infinity separates the Petersburg of the early eighteenth century—a frontier fort on a small island in a forest-lined, untamed river—from the stone, steel, and concrete giant of our times!

The city has had long years of unequal struggle, bright hopes and bitter disappointments. Its people have shed an ocean of tears. But now, the red star of the revolution is proudly displayed on the broad chest of this northern colossus. Once the Tsars' nameless slaves, exhausted by unbearable toil, died here without a murmur. Now their grandchildren and great-grandchildren freely perform unparalleled feats of labour. Once the dry drum-rolls of Paul I's regiments resounded across the city's squares and the whistles of Arakcheyev's rods pierced the city's air. Now the living word is heard; now clear and correct thinking prevails; now the new life of which men have dreamed for centuries is flourishing. Everyone who thinks back through the years will remember days of inspiration and elevation in his life. Such days are priceless, they make life worth living. Leningrad, too, has had such moments. The first was October 1917. The fate of the October Revolution was decided on the streets of Petrograd (as the city was known from 1914 to 1924). Here, the first regiments of the Red Army were formed to defend the new freedom and to vanquish the old world once and for all.

> They blew as always,
> October's
> winds,
> as cold as capitalism
> their icy blast.
> Over Troitsky Bridge
> sped
> cars and trams,
> snaking along
> the rails
> of the past.

These are the words used by the poet Vladimir Mayakovsky to describe the day preceding the onset of the new era ushered in by the storming of the Winter Palace and the victory of the October Revolution. To my mind the most amazing aspect of it all is that for the inhabitants of Petrograd this was a day like any other, "a day as always". There was the usual grey October sky lowering over the city, a sky by now rainless but not yet snow-filled. "Over Troitsky Bridge" (as Kirovsky Bridge was then called) sped automobiles and trams, and thousands upon thousands of people were crossing it as well. . . And many were completely unaware of the turning-point their lives, the life of the country, the life of the world were approaching. Could they have foreseen the future they would have tried to capture and store in their memories every single moment, every minute particular of that day. Most of them, however, knew nothing as yet. . . Or almost nothing. There was a feeling in the air that another collision between revolution and counter-revolution was about to erupt, just "another", not the first, and if not the first, then most likely not the decisive one either. Only Lenin and the Military Revolutionary Committee knew, and the Red Guards, the soldiers and workers already fighting in various parts of the city or massing in the vicinity of the Winter Palace knew or guessed what was about to happen. As evening approached, the autumn gloom solidified. Sinister and ominous stretched the huge expanse of Palace Square; the Winter Palace loomed in the night like a new Bastille. . . With every hour the new day was drawing closer, the first day of a great historic epoch.

It was these historic days that subsequently earned Petrograd its greatest reward: the name "Leningrad", a proud memorial to the greatest Russian—Vladimir Ilyich Lenin.

Our city has long been known as Russia's "window to the West". From 1917, it has been called the cradle of the proletarian revolution. The city's character reflects both: its role as window to the West and its role as first city of the revolution.

The perfection of the city's architecture embodies the best traditions and aspirations of its builders. History and architecture, granite and poetry have become one. Here you will see not only monuments standing on city squares and in the city's buildings; you will see city squares that are themselves monuments, buildings that are monuments, and avenues that are monuments. For it was precisely on them and in them that the history of our great country was played out.

Take, for example, the square in front of Finland Station. No rifle shots or gunfire were heard here. But on April 3, 1917, Lenin, having just returned from exile abroad, uttered his first thunderous words to the workers of Petrograd, to the workers, peasants, and soldiers of the entire country:

"Down with the imperialist war!"

"Long live the socialist revolution!"

Many citizens—most of the intelligentsia, officials, and scientists—knew the name of Lenin, but for them it hardly meant anything. Only the workers and soldiers knew that this name was all-important; it meant their very existence.

A great welcoming crowd gathered in the square in front of Finland Station. Lenin climbed onto the turret of an armoured car and, as he faced the city and, as it were, Russia itself, he proclaimed these slogans, which thundered across the country all the way south to the Black Sea and all the way east to Vladivostok. His words found a response in the heart of every worker and every soldier. They made their way into the countryside, to the millions of uneducated and downtrodden Russian peasants. His words gave them hope for rapid changes, but, most of all, a willingness to go and conquer the future, sparing neither their blood nor their lives.

Now on this square stands a monument to Lenin. Designed by the sculptor Sergei Yevseyev and the architect Vladimir Shchuko, it is probably the only statue in the world whose base is an armoured-car turret, or more accurately, a bronze replica of a turret. In the statue, the artists have managed to capture the historic moment: Lenin standing with his back to the station and to the long years of forced exile he was leaving behind forever. His face and raised arm are turned to his native land, to Russia, to its people and future. This is a remarkable monument to the great revolutionary, the man who literally fashioned a new world, the world of socialism.

Consider yet another of the city's squares—the Field of Mars. It was once a gigantic military parade ground. The wind off the Neva blew in and raised clouds of sand and red dust. Now it is a beautiful garden, flooded in spring by a sea of white and purple lilacs. It is the resting place of the heroes of the February and October revolutions who were buried here in 1917. Two years later, a memorial was erected above their graves. Its granite walls bear solemn epitaphs written by Anatoly Lunacharsky. In the centre burns an eternal flame, which was used to light similar flames at the country's other memorial sites.

This place is lovely by day; enchanting by night, when it is bathed in the light of the garden's many street-lamps; and sadly pensive during the white nights. The Swan Canal flows quietly just to its east, and, beyond it, the marble statues of the Summer Gardens repose in ageless slumber. The Field of Mars is thus an eternal monument to the Revolution as well as one of the most beautiful parts of the city.

Compared to other large cities, Leningrad is a mere youngster, only ninety-odd years older than Washington. Peter the Great founded the city on May 16, 1703. Ten years later, St. Petersburg looked just about as Paris must have looked in the first few centuries A.D., consisting only of an island fortress and a handful of buildings stretching out along the banks of the river. Now Leningrad is not quite three centuries old. Nevertheless, it is one of the ten largest cities in the world.

Youthful cities such as Leningrad seldom acquire "character". This usually takes hundreds, even thousands of years. The same is also true of statues and buildings: the Venus of Milo and the Acropolis would not be quite so interesting if they did not bear the marks of a long, long life. Most cities, too, need time before countless generations can mould their character. The most marvellous thing about Leningrad is that the rule does not hold true. The city was founded fairly recently, and, it may have seemed, in defiance of all reason: that is, on the swampy banks of a wild river, amidst dense forests, and between a sea gulf and an enormous lake, both of which are ice-bound almost half the year. But the city's vital force could not be held in check.

> A century—and the city young,
> Gem of the Northern world, amazing,
> From gloomy wood and swamp upsprung,
> Had risen, in pride and splendour blazing.
>
> (Alexander Pushkin, *The Bronze Horseman.*
> Translated by Oliver Elton)

It is quite understandable that a northern Gibraltar, a major naval base, has grown up here. It is only natural for the noisy docks of a busy trading port to have sprung up here. Nor would it have been surprising if Petersburg, having reached its centenary, had turned into a "central office", a heap of odd structures and administrative buildings needed to rule a colossal empire.

But the beginnings of the new capital coincided with a decisive turning-point in the history of the country. The old Muscovite Russia disappeared, and a new Imperial Russia took its place. A little-known country, which only yesterday had seemed as far away as Asia, took its place among the European powers, moving proudly to the very centre of European life.

It is for this very reason, evidently, that the new city became something quite unique, something of a *Wunderstadt*. In two centuries it had traversed the same stormy and treacherous road it had taken the other world capitals a thousand years to cover.

The city came to maturity—an architectural and poetic gem. I must here allow myself the pleasure of saying that one square kilometre of this city is no less rich aesthetically than any similar area in any of the famous cities of the world and, furthermore, that its aesthetic potential is second to none.

Many of the city's older residents may remember an old, purely Petersburg story.

At the end of the 1850s, an old schooner entered the mouth of the Neva and dropped anchor below the nearest bridge. A small boat then cast off from the schooner and moved upstream. As it passed the place where the Swan Canal flows out of the Neva, it moored. Its owner walked out onto the quay near the gate of the Summer Gardens. He suddenly stopped and stood still, never taking his eyes off the Gardens' famous wrought-iron railings designed by Yury Velten. For no less than an hour he remained rooted to the spot, with a strange look fixed on his face, a look that might well have appeared on Salieri's face as he listened to Mozart, a look of admiration and envy.

He then walked along the fence, turned round, and fell into thought. There were only a few people strolling in the Gardens. One, more curious than the others, came up to him and asked politely, "May I be of service, my dear sir?"

"No!" the man retorted. "It is simply too beautiful. A thousand times more than all the drawings and prints of it I've seen. For many years I've wanted to find out why its charm is so indescribable. Now I can see it myself. Look at the gilded handles on the vases atop its granite pillars. On one vase they turn down, on the two flanking ones they turn up. I'm no Rothschild, but I bought a schooner and sailed here to find out just exactly why this is such a work of genius. Now I know, and there's no reason to stay any longer. Farewell, sir!"

"Adieu, sir!" replied the inquisitive passer-by. It is believed that the latter was the Russian writer Goncharov, but no one really knows for sure.

I have told this story so that the reader can understand what kind of city he will be seeing in this book. The great Dostoyevsky with good reason called it the most contrived, the most fantastical city in the world; and Pushkin, our greatest poet, sang a paean to it in The *Bronze Horseman*, a poetic encyclopaedia of its splendour.

This veritable museum of a city lies on the sixtieth parallel, the same latitude as southern Greenland. If you come to visit us in June, you will probably not manage to fall asleep the first night. You will be waiting for it to get dark, but, even though the sun will set, it will not get any darker. At midnight you can read a book by the window without having to turn on the lights. But it is not really so strange after all; for at 3:45 a.m. the sun will once again appear on the horizon. The entire night, this enchanting white night, will last only five hours and twenty-six minutes. On such a night, the city seems to sink into a silvery-blue haze that comes from nowhere. Lovers will be strolling along the banks of the river. On the stone seats along the quays, university students will be cramming for exams on the resistance of materials and theoretical mechanics. When the school year ends, the happy graduates will dance and sing all night long by the Neva.

Or, if you wish, visit us in winter:

> I love thy ruthless winter, lowering
> With bitter frost and windless air;
> The sledges along Neva scouring;
> Girls' cheeks—no rose so bright and fair!

(Alexander Pushkin, The Bronze Horseman.
Translated by Oliver Elton)

You will not see sledges gliding along the Neva; after all, we live in the age of the automobile! But the "windless air" and "bitter frost" and the rose-red cheeks are still here, along with countless architectural marvels, of which the railings of the Summer Gardens are not the best by far. Don't dawdle, though. The longest December night in Leningrad lasts sixteen hours and fifty-one minutes, while the day lasts only seven hours and nine minutes. On the other hand, night is when the northern lights are sometimes seen.

And so, you are drawing closer to Leningrad. I have no idea how you may come, by land, sea, or air. As for me, I would rather come by sea or air. Each way has its own charm.

If, on some bright morning, you come by ship into the mouth of the Neva, you will already have seen, many miles ahead of you over the low-lying haze of endless buildings, several tall "verticals", as the architects call them. The first to catch your eye will undoubtedly be the relatively low but impressive St. Isaac's Cathedral, whose gold dome rises a hundred metres into the sky, and which was once Russia's main cathedral. A hundred metres is not very tall, but the Neva has so flattened out the land here, at its mouth, that this golden helmet can be seen far away. During the War of 1941–45 (Great Patriotic War), the city's defenders, as they kept watch in their observation posts, could see St. Isaac's in their range-finders and take some cheer from it.

"Old St. Isaac's! It's still standing. Well, we can do it, too!"

During the war, the dome did not shine gold; a grey protective cover had been laid over it. But the main thing is that it stood!

If you take a look through some binoculars, you can see, a little to the left of St. Isaac's, a golden, dagger-like spire. This is the famous Peter and Paul Cathedral. The spire is not only 150 years older than St. Isaac's; it is also twenty-two metres higher. For years, it was considered Europe's highest structure—the spires of the Cologne Cathedral, which are higher, are of later date.

If you look more closely through your binoculars, you will see, side by side with the golden spire, a lacework tower. This is a television tower, a modern structure so light and airy that, even though it is two and a half times taller than the bell-tower of the Peter and Paul Cathedral, it becomes visible only when you get much closer to it.

I have mentioned these three highest points of Leningrad's skyline not for the sake of comparing their dimensions. These structures represent three sharply contrasting epochs in the life of Petersburg–Petrograd–Leningrad. The spire of the Peter and Paul Cathedral dates to the city's infancy, and is thus a symbol of the period when not many people in Russia believed in the city's future, when more believed in its eventual abandonment.

The gold dome of St. Isaac's symbolizes a turning-point in the city's history. It represents the peak in the Romanov's fortunes, yet it also marks the beginning of the end, the beginning of the long descent, which ended so abruptly in 1917.

Finally, the delicate and elegant television tower (316 metres high) is, though perhaps too "utilitarian" when compared to the others, not only the twentieth century and not only the Soviet Union. It is the post-war period, the period of the city's most rapid growth.

If you have chosen to come by air, it is best to come when it's dark. Of course, you have probably flown at dusk or at night into the large cities of the world. You know the shining array of city lights, those constellations and galaxies that twinkle up through the thick fog. Leningrad, too, is a starry firmament come down to earth. Seen from the air, it spreads over its many islands like a gigantic hand, the deep and inky waters of the Neva rushing on between its island fingers. Further to the west, a solid area of black begins—this is the Gulf of Finland.

By day, too, Leningrad is an imposing sight from the air. The Neva may display a whole rainbow of colours—from the deep blue of our golden autumn to the dazzling white of winter. It is fascinating to have a bird's-eye view of this mighty river and builder (indeed, it formed the numerous islands on which Leningrad is built). Later, when you walk along the Neva's quays and stand at the very edge of the water, you can feel the friendly handgrip of this extraordinary river, this half-river, half-strait that connects the huge Lake Ladoga with the Baltic.

While you are still in the air, note one interesting feature. Not one, but two completely different cities lie below you. One is dense and crowds in along the river's banks and on its islands. It comprises broad avenues and narrow streets that fan geometrically out to the east and south-east from the city's heart, the Admiralty. Here, garbed in the raiments of past centuries, the squat houses squeeze together, elbow to elbow; these are the city's venerable centenarians. It is a pleasure to walk along the streets in this section and admire the rich diversity of the façades with their porticos and caryatids. But their courtyards are narrow and dark, and their dimly-lit back stairways are straight out of Zola, Dickens, Nekrasov, or Dostoyevsky. Now they have to be rebuilt. There are many such districts in many of the large cities of the world; like any tourist, you will hardly notice them as you hurry from the Senate (built by Carlo Rossi) to the Admiralty (built by Adrian Zakharov). . .

But all around the city's overcrowded centre stretches yet another city, a new city, which is constantly rising and moving out toward the countryside.

There are no porticos and no caryatids here. Here, as in many modern cities, glass and concrete reign supreme.

The houses no longer fall into endless ranks, as if in obedience to a silent command. The newly built apartment blocks are freely scattered about an area much larger than that of the Petersburg of 1703–1917. These are the houses of the new city, the new Leningrad. This is the city that holds millions of Petersburgers and Leningraders, those that moved here only recently. This is the city ninety per cent of which was built after the war and one hundred per cent of which was built after 1917. Not all the old-time residents like the glass and concrete or the plain geometric lines of the new buildings, similar all over the world, too often lacking character. But when you visit us, remember my advice: try, especially in the evening, to drive slowly through these new residential areas, where the buildings have just been completed and where the occupants are still settling in. Just think: not a single empty flat; all in all, millions of Leningraders! Think about it, and these new areas will no longer seem quite so monotonous. You will come to realize how grand a scale is involved.

There are several cities in Leningrad, each one unique. From the beginning, Leningrad—a naval city with Kronstadt, on Kotlin Island, perched out in front of it—has been a city almost halfway afloat.

Leningrad is a major scientific and research centre. It has a university, several academies, and more than three hundred research institutions and design bureaux.

Leningrad is also a major industrial centre; its large factories, huge wharves, and giant textile mills are no less numerous than its scientific institutions. I remember the early 1900s, when the city's air was thick with coal smoke. Now, after the introduction of gas and electric power, it is cleaner, even though the number of plants and factories has greatly increased.

Leningrad is rich in museums, each one constituting in itself an important architectural monument within this great "museum-city". If you enter Leningrad by sea, the first building you notice will be the Mining Institute designed by Andrei Voronikhin, which stands quite low, just above the level of the water. This amazingly powerful and beautiful edifice can rightly be considered a "temple of science". Its portico is richly decorated with sculptural groups, and in the museum located inside the Institute one can study and appreciate the mineral wealth of Russia.

Another such temple, a "temple of art", is the Russian Museum which holds priceless examples of Russian painting and sculpture. This is Rossi's famous building, regarded as a miracle of architecture not only by its Russian contemporaries, but also by their foreign counterparts. The museum contains superb collections of works of art that testify to the greatness of the Russian creative genius.

Then there is the Academy of Art. This magnificent building was designed by Alexander Kokorinov and Jean-Baptiste Vallin de la Mothe, who created here a supreme example of constructional art. Some years later the architect Thon built a granite landing-stage in front of the Academy of Art, decorating it with bronze lampophores and two Egyptian sphinxes which came from ancient Thebes.

Anyone who comes to visit Leningrad naturally has as its first port of call the Hermitage, the great treasure-house of world art and of the ancient culture of the peoples of our country. At present it occupies the former Winter

Palace and the four buildings traditionally called the Small Hermitage, the Old Hermitage, the New Hermitage, and the Hermitage Theatre. Together they constitute an outstanding architectural ensemble ranging along the Neva.

The Winter Palace was erected between 1754 and 1762 by Bartolommeo Rastrelli in the Baroque style. Between 1764 and 1775, a building of smallish proportions—the Small Hermitage, as they called it afterwards—was designed by Vallin de la Mothe and constructed adjacent to the Winter Palace. The Old Hermitage was built between 1771 and 1787 by Yury Velten to accommodate the ever-growing palace collection of art works. Subsequently Giacomo Quarenghi built the Hermitage Theatre, without doubt one of the most beautiful and harmonious of the buildings that make up the Hermitage ensemble. It was only in the middle of the nineteenth century that the New Hermitage was finally conceived, in a style quite unusual for St. Petersburg. It was designed by Leo von Klenze as a special museum building, and its construction was carried out by Vasily Stasov and Nikolai Yefimov. At its entrance Alexander Terebeniov placed ten powerful granite atlantes, five metres high, and these support the wide balcony overhead.

After the October Revolution the Winter Palace in its entirety was given over to the state as a museum. The scope and variety of the art works which the visitor can see today in the Hermitage can hardly be discussed in detail here. It would be best to go along and see for oneself.

Several magnificent suburbs encircle Leningrad—Pavlovsk, Pushkin, Petrodvorets, and Lomonosov, to name only a few. Each of these Russian Versailles and Fontainebleaus is well worth a visit.

It must, however, be admitted that for all the historic significance of each of these monuments of old, for all the numerous events, grand or tragic, that took place in the splendid palaces, amidst the greenery of the densely treed parks or on the banks of the ponds and tranquil rivulets sung by poets, the Leningrader of today visits most of them simply because he is in love with their beauty.

Of course, the town that bears Pushkin's name (and formerly known as Tsarskoye Selo) is dear to our hearts because of the wondrous genius of Russian poetry who lived here and once said that Tsarskoye Selo would for him forever remain a symbol of the motherland. It is, however, first and foremost their radiant and elegant beauty that lures us to the towns of Pushkin, Gatchina, Pavlovsk, Petrodvorets, and Lomonosov. There is beauty here to suit all tastes. Petrodvorets has its formal parks and its sedate early eighteenth-century architecture; Pavlovsk, its intricately winding rivulets and picturesque dales and hillocks. The architectural genius of Charles Cameron succeeded in creating here a masterpiece of romantic English landscape gardening.

But there is a different type of memorial site too. In Razliv there is the hut and the haystack where Lenin hid out for several days to escape the clutches of the counter-revolutionary Provisional Government.

Now, however, yet another ring encircles the city. It is, with good reason, called the Green Belt of Glory, and it runs along the areas where, between 1941 and 1944, Hitler's armies stood poised to seize Leningrad, where, in January 1944, the near-encirclement was broken through. More than thirty memorials have been raised along this line, amidst quiet fields and forests, where forty years ago the roar of explosions was deafening, smoke was swirling up, and people were dying. For 900 days and nights the people of Leningrad stood their ground, refusing to let the most horrendous blockade of all times strangle their city.

Even many books cannot do justice to the road that Leningrad has passed; nor can a whole gallery of paintings capture the many faces of the city. But each new word and every new photograph, if offered with love and truth, will add something to what we should know about the city. This book will have succeeded if it enables the people of Leningrad to look at their city anew and if it allows the first-time visitor to get acquainted with this wondrous city. This city—the city of Lenin, the city of the revolution, the heroic city of the war—deserves all the love that people have for it.

Lev Uspensky

Leningrad

1   The Peter and Paul Fortress from the Spit of Vasilyevsky Island

2   The Peter and Paul Fortress

3   Interior of the Cathedral of Sts Peter and Paul

Cathedral of Sts Peter and Paul

5–13   Views of the Peter and Paul Fortress

14   Section of the Peter and Paul Fortress. Aerial view

15   Lamp on St. John's Bridge

На этом месте
13/25 июля 1826 года
были казнены
декабристы
П. Пестель
К. Рылеев
П. Каховский
С. Муравьев-Апостол
М. Бестужев-Рюмин

16, 17   Memorial slabs on the Decembrists' place of execution (1826)

18   Nigh-time in the Peter and Paul Fortress

19   The Peter and Paul Fortress. A former prison cell in the Trubetskoi Bastion

Kirovsky Bridge over the Neva

22   Allegorical statue of Suvorov

НЕ ЖЕРТВЫ · ГЕРОИ
ЛЕЖАТ ПОД ЭТОЙ МОГИЛОЙ
НЕ ГОРЕ А ЗАВИСТЬ
РОЖДАЕТ СУДЬБА ВАША
В СЕРДЦАХ
ВСЕХ БЛАГОДАРНЫХ
ПОТОМКОВ
В КРАСНЫЕ СТРАШНЫЕ ДНИ
СЛАВНО ВЫ ЖИЛИ
И УМИРАЛИ ПРЕКРАСНО

23   A stela of the Memorial to the Fallen Heroes of the Revolution on the Field of Mars

Leningrad Branch of the Central Lenin Museum (the former Marble Palace)

26   Memorial Armoured Car in the courtyard of the Lenin Museum

Museum of the October Revolution from the courtyard

6ДМ БАКОВОЕ ОРУДИЕ
ИЗ КОТОРОГО ПРОИЗВЕДЕН
ИСТОРИЧЕСКИЙ ВЫСТРЕЛ
25 ОКТЯБРЯ 1917г. В МОМЕНТ
ВЗЯТИЯ ЗИМНЕГО ДВОРЦА.
КРЕЙСЕР „АВРОРА" 1927г.

29–32   On board the cruiser *Aurora*

The cruiser *Aurora*, memorial of the October Revolution

IN THE DAYS
OF THE 1917 OCTOBER REVOLUTION,
SMOLNY BECAME THE HEADQUARTERS
OF THE ARMED WORKERS,
SOLDIERS, AND SAILORS.
FROM HERE
LENIN PERSONALLY DIRECTED
THE OCTOBER UPRISING.

Statue of Lenin in front of Smolny

36   Smolny. Lenin's desk

37   Smolny. Part of Lenin's reception room

Proletarian Dictatorship Square with the building of the Executive Committee of the Smolninsky District of People's Deputies

40   Statue of Dzerzhinsky

41   Bird's-eye view of the Tauride Palace ensemble

42   The White-columned Hall in the Tauride Palace

Bird's-eye view of the Smolny ensemble

45   Branch of the Museum of the History of Leningrad (the former Cathedral of the Smolny Convent)

The Spit of Vasilyevsky Island

47   Sculpture at the base of a rostral column

49   Central Naval Museum (the former Stock Exchange building)

Neptune, a sculptural group decorating the Stock Exchange building

51   The Spit of Vasilyevsky Island by night

The USSR Academy of Sciences building and the former *Kunstkammer*

53   Seagull on the granite parapet of the Neva embankment

55, 56   Equestrian statue of Peter the Great (The Bronze Horseman) on Decembrists' Square

57   The Neva on a windy day

Central Historical Archives (the former Senate and Synod buildings) on Decembrists' Square

59   Archway linking the former Senate and Synod buildings

Top of the column with the statue of Victory on Boulevard Profsoyuzov

Granite columns of St. Isaac's Cathedral

65–73   Glimpses of St. Isaac's Square

74   Bird's-eye view of St. Isaac's Square with St. Isaac's Cathedral in the centre

Rotunda in the former Mariinsky Palace

Building of the Executive Committee of the Leningrad City Soviet of People's Deputies (the former Mariinsky Palace)

77   Entrance hall of the Admiralty

78   Central portion of the Admiralty

79   Detail of the sculptural group crowning the arch of the former General Staff building

81   Bird's-eye view of Palace Square

82   Detail of the sculptural group crowning the arch of the former General Staff building

ON THE NIGHT
OF OCTOBER 25 (NOVEMBER 7), 1917,
THE WINTER PALACE—
RESIDENCE OF THE TSARS
AND SEAT OF THE LAST GOVERNMENT
OF THE BOURGEOISIE—
WAS TAKEN BY STORM BY RED GUARDSMEN
AND REVOLUTIONARY UNITS
OF THE ARMY AND NAVY.

83   Palace Square. Arch of the former General Staff building

The Hermitage. North façade of the Winter Palace

85   The Main Staircase in the Winter Palace

86   The Leonardo Room in the Hermitage

87 The *Litta Madonna* by Leonardo da Vinci

88   Room of 17th- and 18th-century Italian painting in the Hermitage

91   The White Dining-hall in the Winter Palace, where the ministers of the Provisional Government were arrested in 1917

92   *Still Life with Attributes of the Arts* by Jean-Baptiste Chardin

121–125   Works of applied art from the Hermitage

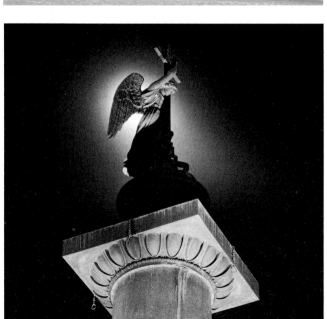

126—134   Glimpses of the Hermitage buildings and Palace Square

135 Base of the Alexander Column on Palace Square

137   The Moika near Pevchesky Bridge

138   Railings of Pevchesky Bridge

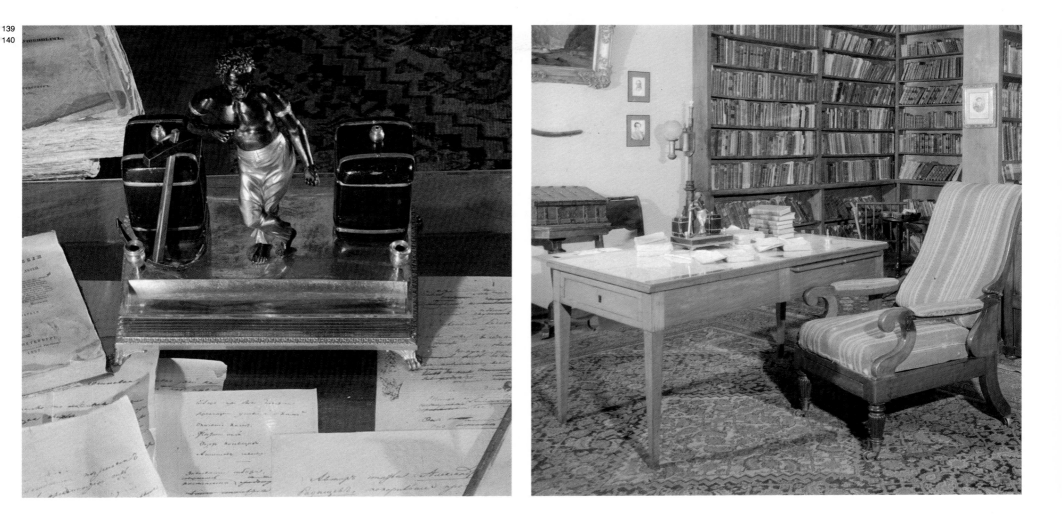

139, 140   The Pushkin Memorial Museum on the Moika Embankment. The poet's study

153 The Summer Gardens. *Peace and Abundance*

154   Avenue in the Summer Gardens

155   Detail of the Summer Gardens' railings

156   The Summer Gardens. *Bellona*

157   Detail of Second Sadovy Bridge's railings

158   First Sadovy Bridge over the Moika. In the distance, the Rossi Pavilion in the Mikhailovsky Garden

160 Equestrian statue of Peter the Great in front of the Engineers' (Mikhailovsky) Castle 161 Bas-relief on the pediment of the Engineers' (Mikhailovsky) Castle

162   Bird's-eye view of the Engineers' (Mikhailovsky) Castle and the Field of Mars

163   The Russian Museum (the former Mikhailovsky Palace)

Statue of Pushkin on Arts Square

A Russian Scaevola by Vasily Demuth-Malinovsky

166   Entrance hall of the Russian Museum

167
168
169

170
171
172

173
174
175

176
177
178

167–178   Masterpieces of art from the Russian Museum

179   The Archangel Gabriel ("The Golden-haired Angel")

180   *Portrait of Sarah Fermore* by Ivan Vishniakov

181   The White Hall in the Russian Museum

182   Lion adorning the main entrance to the Russian Museum

The Russian Museum from the Mikhailovsky Garden

Sculptural group adorning the Museum of the Ethnography of the Peoples of the USSR

185–188   Arts Square

185   The Academic Maly Theatre of Opera and Ballet

187   Museum of the Ethnography of the Peoples of the USSR

186   Detail of the Maly Theatre's façade

188   Grand Concert Hall of the Leningrad Philharmonic Society

189   Courtyard of the former Stroganov Palace

The former Stroganov Palace from the Moika

ГРАЖДАНЕ!
ПРИ АРТОБСТРЕЛЕ
ЭТА СТОРОНА УЛИЦЫ
НАИБОЛЕЕ ОПАСНА

В ПАМЯТЬ О ГЕРОИЗМЕ И МУЖЕСТВЕ
ЛЕНИНГРАДЦЕВ В ДНИ 900-ДНЕВНОЙ
БЛОКАДЫ ГОРОДА СОХРАНЕНА ЭТА
НАДПИСЬ.

191   A memorial plaque on a Leningrad house (No. 14, Nevsky Prospekt) reminding of the War of 1941—45
when the city was subjected to severe shelling

193–201   Glimpses of Nevsky Prospekt

193	Vosstania Square	194	Sculptural group topping the House of Books	195	Catholic Church of St. Catherine
196	Central part of the Gostiny Dvor (shopping arcades)	197	Lutheran Church	198	Brodsky Street with the Russian Museum in the distance
199	Entrance to the Nevsky Prospekt Metro Station	200	Building of the former State Duma	201	Moskow Railway Station

202   Museum of the History of Religion and Atheism (the former Cathedral of Our Lady of Kazan). Statue of Kutuzov

203   The Cathedral of Our Lady of Kazan. Partial view of the dome

A chandelier in the Cathedral of Our Lady of Kazan

205   Colonnade of the Cathedral of Our Lady of Kazan. In the distance, the House of Books

207–210   Leningrad by night

The Pushkin Drama Theatre. Monument to Catherine II

Sculptural group surmounting the pediment of the Pushkin Drama Theatre

215   Book-stack in the Saltykov-Shchedrin Public Library

216   Kuibyshevsky District Committee of the CPSU (the former Palace of the Counts Beloselsky-Belozersky) in Nevsky Prospekt

217   The Palace of Young Pioneers (the former Anichkov Palace)

One of the four *Horse Taming* sculptural groups decorating Anichkov Bridge

219   Anichkov Bridge over the Fontanka

The Fontanka by night

222–230   Banks of the Fontanka

222 Detail of the gates of the Sheremetev Palace	223 Church of St. Pantaleon	224 The Fontanka near the Summer Gardens
225 The Sheremetev Palace	226 Lamp on Lomonosov Bridge	227 The Gorky Drama Theatre
228 Lomonosov Bridge	229 The House of Friendship and Peace (the former Shuvalov Palace)	230 Lomonosov Square

231 Detail of Egyptian Bridge with Hotel Sovetskaya in the background

232   The House of Friendship and Peace (the former Shuvalov Palace). The Gilt Drawing-room

233   The House of Friendship and Peace (the former Shuvalov Palace). The Mauve Drawing-room

234   Bank Bridge over the Griboyedov Canal

235–243   Views of the Griboyedov Canal banks

The Dostoyevsky Memorial Museum. The writer's study

246   Archway in an Art-Nouveau apartment house on the Fontanka Embankment

The Fontanka Embankment by night

The Blok Memorial Museum. The poet's study

249   Lions' Bridge over the Griboyedov Canal

251   Auditorium of the Kirov Opera and Ballet Theatre

252   The "New Holland" Arch

253   Footbridge over the Moika

255   Lamp decorating the portico of the Palace of Labour

The Academy of Art. Vestibule on the first floor

258   The Academy of Art. Entrance hall on the ground floor

259   The University Embankment near the Academy of Art

260   Detail of a sphinx decorating the landing-stage in front of the Academy of Art

261
262
263

264
265
266

267
268
269

261–269 Vasilyevsky Island

261 Statue of Admiral Krusenstern
264 Institute of Russian Literature (known as Pushkin House) of the USSR Academy of Sciences
267 Church of St. Catherine

262 The Mining Institute
265 Detail of a bronze lampophore decorating the landing-stage in front of the Academy of Art
268 Arcade of Leningrad University

263 Sailing vessels
266 The Rumiantsev Obelisk
269 Scene on the Neva

270   Leningrad University (the former Twelve Collegia building)

271   Branch of the Hermitage (the former Menshikov Palace)

272   Entrance hall of the Menshikov Palace

The Walnut Study in the Menshikov Palace

274   Volodarsky Bridge over the Neva

Dvortsovy Bridge on a white night

276   TV tower

277   Hotel Leningrad

279   Sculptural group decorating the entrance to the Oktiabrsky Concert Hall

280   The Lenin Memorial in Razliv

282   Gulf of Finland

281   Finland Station. Steam locomotive No. 293
which brought Lenin to revolutionary Petrograd

283   "The Hut" Memorial in Razliv

Monument to Lenin in front of Finland Station

285, 286   The former Bezborodko villa

287   An Art-Nouveau apartment house on Leo Tolstoy Square

288–296   Glimpses of Petrogradskaya Side

288   Cottage of Peter the Great

291   Monument to the Heroic Sailors of the
Destroyer *Steregushchy*

294   The Yubileiny Sports Palace

289   Interior of the Cottage of Peter the Great

292   Lamp on Kirovsky Bridge

295   Statue of Maxim Gorky

290   Petrovskaya Embankment on a festive day

293   Apartment house on the Karpovka Embankment

296   The Palace of Youth

Chornaya Rechka Metro Station

298   Statue of Pushkin in the hall of the Chornaya Rechka Metro Station   299   Bank of the Chornaya Rechka. Obelisk on the site of Pushkin's duel

301   Suite of rooms in the Yelagin Palace

304   Bird's-eye view of Moskovskaya Square with the statue of Lenin

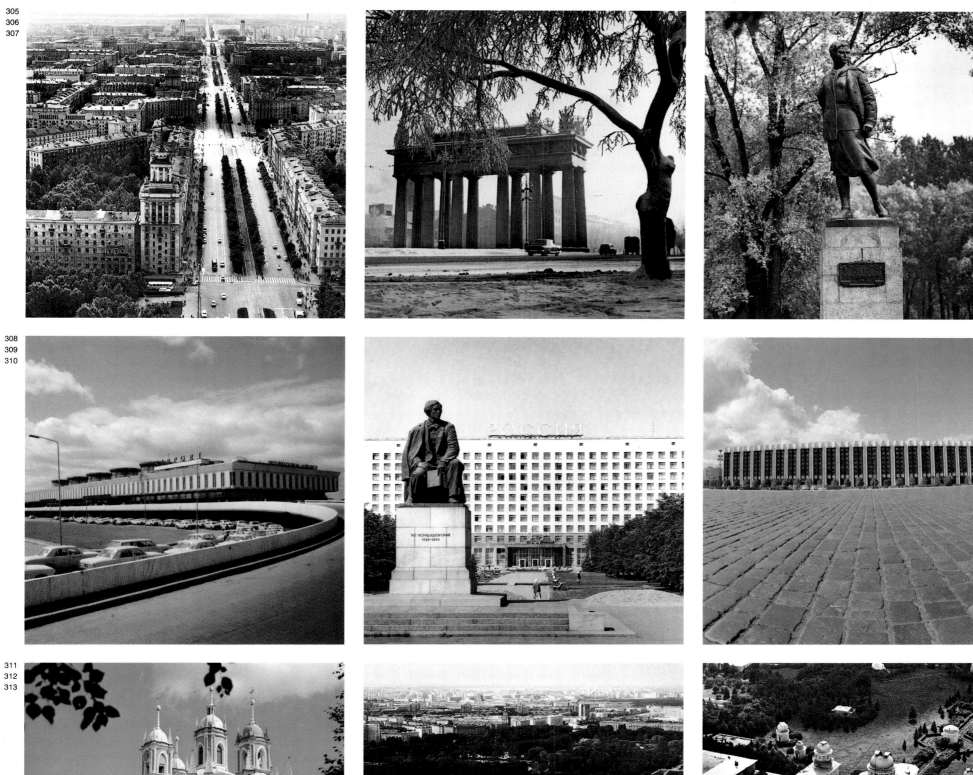

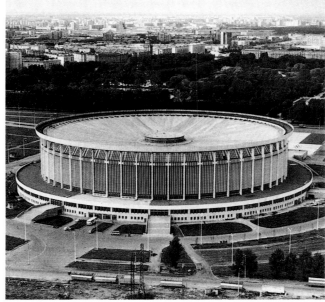

314   *The Victors*: central sculptural group of the Memorial to the Heroic Defenders of Leningrad

315   General view of the Memorial to the Heroic Defenders of Leningrad on Victory Square

316   *The Broken Ring*: part of the Memorial to the Heroic Defenders of Leningrad

317   *The Blockade*: sculptural group of the Memorial to the Heroic Defenders of Leningrad

Detail of the Memorial to the Heroic Defenders of Leningrad

319
320

319   Pill-box, one of the war relics making part of the Green Belt of Glory

320   Milestone on the Road of Life, one of the memorials of the Green Belt of Glory

321   *The Broken Ring*, one of the memorials of the Green Belt of Glory, symbolizing the lifting of the siege of Leningrad

322   Tombstone over a mass grave in the Piskariovskoye Memorial Cemetery

Flame of Remembrance in the Piskariovskoye Memorial Cemetery

324–328 Piskariovskoye Memorial Cemetery

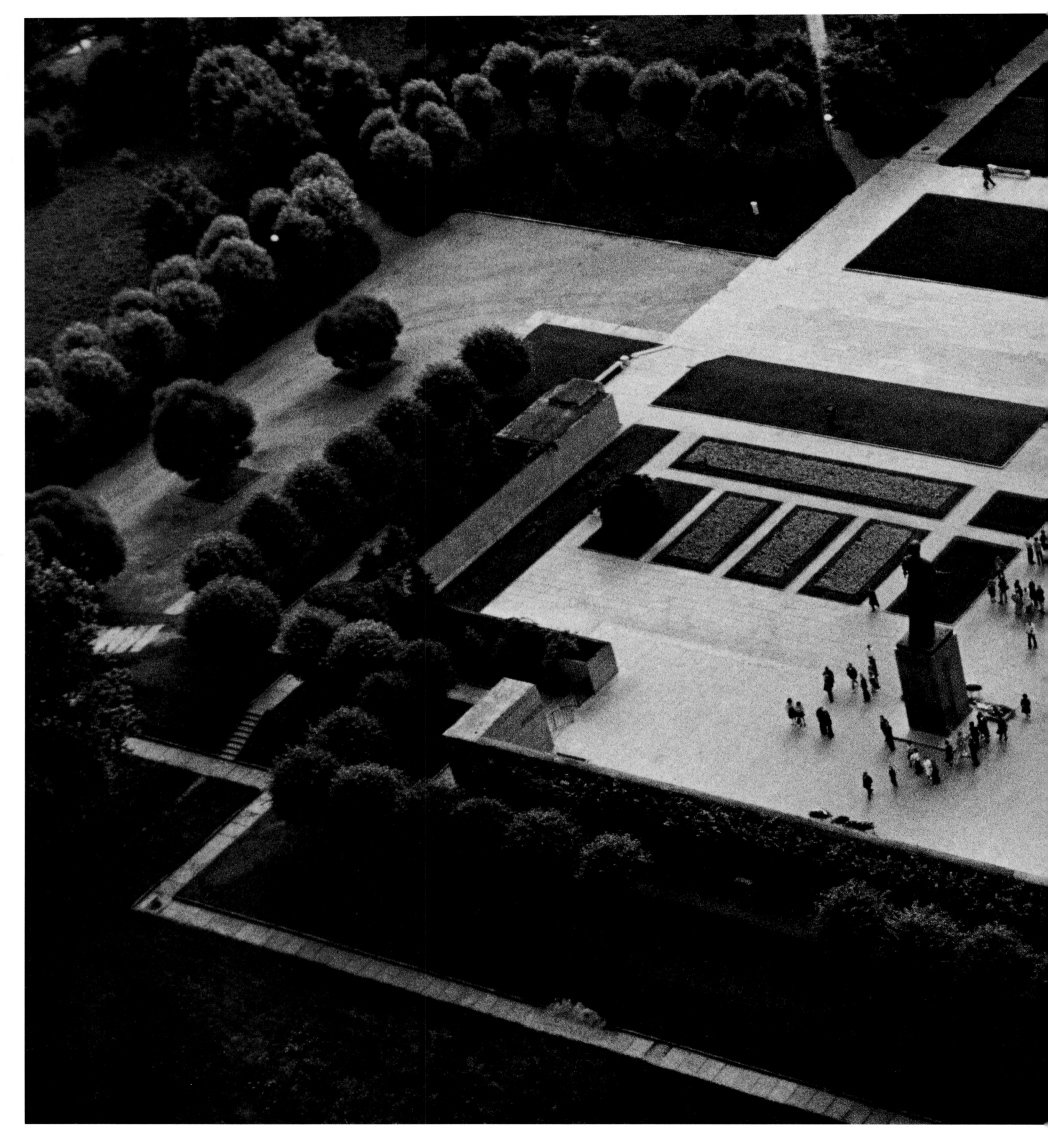

329   Bird's-eye view of the Piskariovskoye Memorial Cemetery

330–347   Views of new Leningrad

330	New block of Leningrad University	331	Blocks of flats near Victory Square	332	Ploshchad Muzhestva Metro Station
333	New residential district	334	Theatre for Young People	335	*Sovremennik* Cinema
336	Sverdlovskaya Embankment	337	Modern apartment house in Sestroretsk	338	New residential area in the south-west (Pionerstroi Street)

Sculptural group in front of Hotel Pribaltiyskaya

351   Partial view of the Port Arrival and Departure building

Seafront of Leningrad

353   The Gulf of Finland

Petrodvorets
Lomonosov
Pushkin
Pavlovsk

Panorama of Petrodvorets with the Great Palace and Upper Gardens

355　The Great Cascade

356　The Samson fountain

357   Fountain jet

358   The Great Cascade. *Actaeon*. Detail

The Great Cascade and Sea Canal on a festive night

360–368   Views of Petrodvorets

360	Bird's-eye view of the Upper Gardens	361	The Sirens fountain	362	Statue of Apollo
363	Parterre with sculptures	364	Mascaron of the Marble Bench fountain	365	The Adam fountain
366	The Hermitage Pavilion	367	The Sun fountain	368	The Cottage Pavilion

370   The Throne Room in the Great Palace

371   The Western Chinese Lobby in the Great Palace

The Picture Room in the Great Palace

373   The Sea Canal seen from the Great Palace

374 The Chessboard Hill Cascade   375 Dragons decorating the Chessboard Hill Cascade

376 The Roman fountain   377 Base of the Pyramid fountain

379   The Marly Palace

381   The Monplaisir Palace

380   Interior view of the Marly Palace

382   Terrace of the Monplaisir Palace with the statue of Neptune

383–391   Palaces and Parks of Lomonosov

	384 Statue of Venus de' Medici near the Chinese Palace
383 Entrance gates of the Peterstadt fortress	387 Painted ceiling of the Big
386 The Big Chinese Study in the Chinese Palace	Chinese Study in the Chinese Palace
389 Palace of Peter III	390 The Grand Hall in the Chinese Palace

385   Decorative detail of the Coasting Hill Pavilion

388   Petrovsky Bridge

391   The Buglework Room in the Chinese Palace

Lomonosov. South façade of the Chinese Palace

393   The Hall of the Muses in the Chinese Palace

394   Sculptural figure of Jonah with the Pergola in the distance

395   The Study in the Palace of Peter III

397   The Coasting Hill Pavilion

398   The Circular Hall in the Coasting Hill Pavilion

399 Pushkin. The Lyceum

400 Monument to Pushkin in the Lyceum Garden

401   Parterre in front of the Great (Catherine) Palace

403   The Green Dining-room in the Catherine Palace

404   The Main Staircase in the Catherine Palace

405   The Cesme Column in the Catherine Park

416   Colonnade of the Cameron Gallery

417   Grille of the Grotto Pavilion

The Grotto Pavilion in the Catherine Park

419   Marble (Siberian) or Palladian Bridge in the Catherine Park

420 Bench in the Catherine Park

421 *Girl with a Pitcher* fountain in the Catherine Park

422   The Ruin-Kitchen Pavilion in the Alexander Park

423   The Gothic Gates in the Alexander Park

424   The Concert Hall in the Catherine Park in winter

425   The Pavlovsk Palace

426   The Egyptian Vestibule in the Pavlovsk Palace

The Picture Gallery in the Pavlovsk Palace

428   The annular clock in the Tapestry Room of the Pavlovsk Palace

429   The Little Lantern in the Pavlovsk Palace

430 Mantelpiece mirror in the Old Drawing-room of the Pavlovsk Palace

431   The Grecian Hall in the Pavlovsk Palace

432   The Apollo Colonnade in the Pavlovsk Park

433–441   Views of the Pavlovsk Park

433	The Three Graces Pavilion	434	The Aviary	435	The Peel Tower
436	Lion decorating the Great Stone Stairway	437	The Great Stone Stairway	438	The statue of Peace
439	New Sylvia Bridge	440	Bridge over the Ruin Cascade	441	Apollo Belvedere

442   The Great Palace with Centaur Bridge in the foreground

Detail of Centaur Bridge

445   Statue of Terpsichore

Brief Data
on the Architectural History
of Leningrad

2–20 The Peter and Paul Fortress

The cornerstone of this outstanding historic and architectural monument was laid on May 16 (27, New Style), 1703, and it is from this day that the city dates its existence.

The first fortress was an earthwork structure. It was rebuilt in stone under the supervision of Domenico Trezzini who also designed a number of buildings within its walls, among them the Cathedral of Sts Peter and Paul.

The fortress is in plan a hexagon stretched out from west to east. The bell-tower of the Cathedral of Sts Peter and Paul is one of the tallest architectural points of the city.

Access to the fortress from Revolution Square is through St. John's Gate, put up in the 1740s, and through the old St. Peter's Gate designed by Trezzini. Preserved intact on the territory of the fortress are structures dating from the 18th and 19th centuries.

In the 18th century, the fortress was turned into a political prison. Its walls saw several generations of Russian revolutionaries—Radishchev, the Decembrists, Chernyshevsky, the *Narodnaya Volia* (People's Will) heroes and Leninist Bolsheviks. Incarcerated in the cells of the Trubetskoi Bastion were Zheliabov, a founding member of the People's Will Party; Lenin's elder brother Alexander Ulyanov; Lenin's associates—Olminsky, Lepeshinsky, Baumann; the writer Maxim Gorky, and others. The Peter and Paul Fortress played an important role in the crucial days of October 1917 when its garrison went over to the side of the revolution.

The Cathedral of Sts Peter and Paul took 21 years to build—from 1712 to 1733. It has a hipped roof and a cupola of modest dimensions over the altar; in plan it is an elongated rectangle. The western portion of the cathedral, decorated with a portal, serves as a base for a bell-tower surmounted by a spire. The height of the bell-tower, spire and all, is 122.5 metres.

The interior of the cathedral resembles a palace hall. The lofty vaults rest on massive piers which partition off the interior into a nave and two aisles. The nave leads to an altar with a carved wooden iconostasis designed in the shape of a triumphal gate by Ivan Zarudny. Constructed in Moscow in the 1720s, the iconostasis is an incomparable example of Russian wood-carving.

After the October Revolution the fortress was transformed into a museum (a section of the Museum of the History of Leningrad) dedicated to the heroism of Russian revolutionaries.

Opposite the cathedral is a little pavilion, the so-called Boathouse, built in 1763 to the design of Alexander Wist to house "the grandfather of the Russian Navy"—the boat of Peter the Great (now in the Central Naval Museum).

22 Allegorical statue of Suvorov

The famous Russian field marshal is presented by Mikhail Kozlovsky in the image of Mars, the god of war. The circular pedestal designed jointly with Andrei Voronikhin is embellished with a bronze bas-relief by Fiodor Gordeyev. All the bronze parts of the monument were cast by the smelter Vasily Yekimov.

The monument was unveiled on May 5 (17, New Style), 1801.

23, 24 The Field of Mars

This open plot of ground used to be called at different times the Great Meadow, the Amusement Field (because of "amusement lights" or fire-crackers set off here during court festivities), and the Tsarina's Meadow (because Catherine I's palace was situated close by). Later it came to be called the Field of Mars because of the military parades and reviews held here from the late 18th century onwards.

In the 18th and 19th centuries, several imposing buildings were erected on the Field's periphery: the Marble Palace, now the Leningrad Branch of the Central Lenin Museum, by Antonio Rinaldi (1768–85); the mansion of Field Marshal Nikolai Saltykov, now the Krupskaya Institute of Culture, by Giacomo Quarenghi (1784–88); the Barracks of the Pavlovsky Regiment of the Guards, now the Lenenergo building, by Vasily Stasov (1817–19), and others.

In 1917, the fallen heroes of the February and October revolutions were buried here; in 1918, Volodarsky and Uritsky, assassinated by socialist-revolutionary terrorists, as well as Petrograd workers who died in Yaroslavl defending the socialist cause against counter-revolutionary armed insurrection.

On November 7, 1919, in the centre of the Field of Mars, a memorial ensemble was unveiled, dedicated to the heroes of the revolution. This memorial by Lev Rudnev is one of the most significant achievements of Soviet monumental art. Carved on its granite walls are epitaphs composed by Anatoly Lunacharsky, the first People's Commissar for Education.

Lenin, accompanied by delegates to the Second Congress of the Comintern, visited the Field of Mars in July 1920.

In 1957, on the eve of the 40th anniversary of the October Revolution, an eternal flame was lit here. The dark-grey granite platform and burner were designed by E. Maiofis.

25, 26 Leningrad Branch of the Central Lenin Museum (the former Marble Palace)

Designed by Antonio Rinaldi and erected between 1768 and 1785, this palace stands out for its strict forms and restrained décor. The two upper storeys with their unhurried alternation of pilasters of the Corinthian order are faced with marble and light-grey granite; the raised ground floor, with pink granite. The central part of the façade is crowned by an attic ornamented with decorative vases and two statues by Fedot Shubin. In 1844–51 the palace's interior was redesigned by Alexander Briullov. Only the Grand Staircase retained its original aspect and, in part, the Grand Hall with its bas-reliefs by Mikhail Kozlovsky and Shubin.

In 1937, the palace was given over to the Central Lenin Museum. In the inner garden of the palace is an armoured car with the words *The Enemy of Capital* inscribed on its turret. It is from this improvised stand that Lenin addressed a huge crowd of workers, soldiers, and sailors outside Finland Station on April 3 (16, New Style), 1917.

The museum has a rich collection of artifacts and documents relating to the life and revolutionary activities of Lenin.

27, 28 Museum of the October Revolution

The museum was organized in 1919. Its present exhibition has been on view since 1957, when the country was celebrating the 40th anniversary of the Soviet state.

Part of the museum's exhibits are housed in the former Kshesinskaya mansion (built in 1906 by A. Hogen), which from March to July 1917 served as the headquarters of the Central and Petrograd Committees of the Bolshevik Party. This is the house Lenin first came to on his return to Russia from abroad on April 3 (16, New Style), 1917, and it is from the balcony of this mansion that he repeatedly addressed the workers, soldiers, and sailors of Petrograd.

The Museum of the October Revolution, with over 7,000 exhibits on display in its halls, is a veritable treasure-house of revolutionary relics.

29–33 The Cruiser *Aurora*

Designed by Tokarevsky, the cruiser entered service with the Russian Navy in 1903. In 1905, it took part in the battle of Tsushima Strait; in 1909, became a training-ship; during World War I, from 1914 to 1916, operated in the Baltic. In the February revolution of 1917 the *Aurora* hoisted a red flag to express its support for the people's struggle. On October 25 (November 7, New Style), 1917, the cruiser, acting in accordance with Lenin's plan for armed uprising, approached Nikolayevsky Bridge (now Lt. Schmidt Bridge) on the Neva and aimed its guns at the Winter Palace. At 9:45 p.m. it fired the historic shot that signalled the storming of the Winter Palace.

From 1923 the *Aurora* served as a training-ship for future officers of the Soviet Navy. Anchored in the vicinity of Lomonosov during the War of 1941–45, it was a link in the chain of anti-aircraft defences around Leningrad.

On November 17, 1948, the *Aurora*, a revered relic of the October Revolution, was moored permanently in the Bolshaya Nevka opposite the Nakhimov Naval School. In 1965, the cruiser received the status of a branch of the Central Naval Museum.

34–38 Smolny

This is a world-famous monument, the headquarters of the October Revolution that is forever linked with the name of Lenin.

It was built in 1806–8 by Giacomo Quarenghi to house a boarding-school for young ladies of noble birth. The name, Smolny, goes back to the early 18th century when a tar-yard (*smolianoi dvor*) was located here which stored tar for the city's shipyards.

The Smolny building is a splendid example of early 19th-century Classicism. An octastyle portico adorns the central part of the main façade above the ground-floor arcade. A broad staircase leads to the main entrance. The interiors are spacious and very simply decorated. The Assembly Hall of Smolny is one of the finest examples of its kind in Russian architecture.

The summer of 1917 opened a new chapter in the history of the edifice: on August 4 (17, New Style), the All-Russia Central Executive Committee and the Petrograd Soviet of Workers' and Soldiers' Deputies moved here from the Tauride Palace. In October, the Central

Committee of the Bolshevik Party reached a decision in favour of armed uprising, and its Military and Revolutionary Committee began working in Smolny.

On October 24 (November 6, New Style), 1917, Lenin left his last underground lodgings in Serdobolskaya Street and came to Smolny to head the uprising of the armed proletariat. Smolny became the headquarters of the socialist revolution. From here Lenin supervised and directed the October uprising from start to finish, including the assault and capture of the bourgeois Provisional Government's last stronghold—the Winter Palace. By the morning of October 25 (November 7) all the strategic points of Petrograd were in the hands of the armed masses—the post office, the telegraph office, the radio station, the Neva bridges, the railway stations and the National Bank. Later in the day Lenin addressed an emergency session of the Petrograd Soviet in the Assembly Hall of Smolny with the historic words: "The workers' and peasants' revolution, the need of which the Bolsheviks have stressed time and again, has happened..." When the *Aurora* fired its historic shot, the Second All-Russia Congress of Soviets was in session in the Assembly Hall of Smolny. The sittings were continued in the evening of October 26, and the Congress adopted the first decrees, proposed by Lenin, of the new régime—the Decree on Peace and the Decree on the Land. The Congress also approved the formation of the first ever workers' and peasants' government, the Council of People's Commissars, with Lenin at its head.

Smolny remained the seat of the Soviet Government till March 10, 1918.

Situated on the second floor of the building is Lenin's former study. On the first floor of the west wing is the little room which Lenin and Krupskaya occupied from mid-November till the government moved to Moscow. Today all this is part of the Lenin Memorial Museum.

In 1927, a statue of Lenin was set up in front of the portico (sculptor Vasily Kozlov, architect Vladimir Shchuko). The entrance to the tree-lined avenue leading from Proletarian Dictatorship Square to Smolny is flanked with propylaea put up in 1924 to the design of Shchuko and Helfreich. They bear the inscriptions "The First Soviet of the Proletarian Dictatorship" and "Workers of All Countries, Unite!" On the grass plots in front of Smolny stand the busts of Karl Marx and Friedrich Engels by Sergei Yevseyev.

39 Proletarian Dictatorship Square

The once neglected grounds opposite Smolny were converted into Proletarian Dictatorship Square. In 1974, the House of Political Studies was built here. A group of architects supervised by D. Goldgor, responsible for its construction, succeeded in attuning it to a neighbouring administrative building erected in 1957 to the design of D. Goldgor and S. Podlesnova.

The ensemble of the square was completed in 1980 with the construction of the building of the Executive Committee of the Smolninsky District Soviet of People's Deputies on the southern part of the square.

40 Statue of Dzerzhinsky

Felix Dzerzhinsky (1877–1926), Polish and Russian revolutionary; since 1917, Head of the All-Russia Special Commission for Combatting Counter-revolution, Sabotage, and Speculation (the Cheka).

The statue, designed by V. Gorevoi and S. Kubasov, was unveiled in 1981.

41–43 The Tauride Palace

Built between 1783 and 1789 by Ivan Starov, the Tauride Palace, a remarkable example of the Classical style, is one of the most interesting architectural and historical monuments of Leningrad. The general impression is one of compositional clarity and simplicity. The central two-storey block is crowned by a low dome and connected by single-storey galleries with the two-storey pavilions. The main entrance is decorated with a hexastyle portico in the centre of the façade. The smooth walls of the central block are transpierced by tall windows and surmounted by an entablature with a frieze of triglyphs. The austere simplicity of the façade is offset, as it were, by the solemn splendour of the interior décor. The vestibule leads into a rotunda which is connected with a magnificent columned hall.

The Tauride Palace is associated with some of the major events of the February and October revolutions. It was here that on April 4 (17, New Style), 1917, Lenin read out his famous April theses at a meeting of Bolshevik delegates to the All-Russia Conference of Soviets of Workers' and Soldiers' Deputies.

At present the palace houses the Higher School of Party Education.

44, 45 Branch of the Museum of the History of Leningrad (Cathedral of the former Smolny Convent)

Designed by Bartolommeo Rastrelli, this is an outstanding example of Russian architecture in the mid-18th century. Its construction was begun in 1748 and completed in the rough in 1764. The final stage of the construction and the interior decoration were effected by Vasily Stasov in 1832–35.

The complex and dynamic design of the façades with sculptures and stucco mouldings, the clusters of columns decorating the corners, the richly adorned window surrounds, and the broken semicircular pediments over the doorways are all typical of 18th-century Baroque. The elegance and sumptuousness of the architectural décor go hand in hand here with a monumentality that stems from the building's perfect proportions. When Stasov brought the structure to completion, he designed the interiors in the style of Late Classicism.

46 The Spit of Vasilyevsky Island

After the founding of St. Petersburg, Peter the Great planned to turn the entire large Elk Island, later renamed Vasilyevsky, into the capital's new administrative and commercial centre. In the northern part of the island's spit a commercial port was built, in the southern part, the *Kunstkammer*.

The Stock Exchange building (now Central Naval Museum), which later became the centrepiece of the architectural ensemble of the Spit, was erected by Thomas de Thomon in the early 19th century. Two rostral columns, an integral part of the projected ensemble, were put up in 1810.

The Customs House (now Institute of Russian Literature), another noteworthy feature of the Spit, was designed by Giovanni Luchini and erected in 1829–32. In the second half of the 19th century, the port was transferred to the Neva's estuary.

Now a number of museums and research institutes are housed in the buildings composing the architectural ensemble of the Spit of Vasilyevsky Island.

47 The Rostral Columns

The two monumental rostral columns of the Doric order stand on the very edge of the embankment as it slopes down to the Neva, one on each side of the semicircular area fronting the Stock Exchange building. The columns, an integral part of de Thomon's projected ensemble, were put up in 1810. They were intended to serve as beacons and to stress the dominant role of the Exchange in the life of St. Petersburg's port. The bases of the rostral columns are grey granite, and the columns themselves are built of blocks of Pudost stone and decorated with ship's prows.

Installed on the columns are cup-like burners resting on tripods, and on festive days huge tongues of flame rise skyward from their tops.

The rostral columns are a magnificent example of a synthesis of architecture and sculpture. The giant figures in Pudost stone at the bases of the columns symbolize four Russian rivers—the Volga, the Dnieper, the Neva, and the Volkhov. They were designed by an anonymous artist and carved out of stone by Samson Sukhanov.

49, 50 Central Naval Museum (the former Stock Exchange building)

This building is the pivot of the splendid architectural ensemble on the Spit of Vasilyevsky Island. It was erected in 1805–10 by Thomas de Thomon as the main building of the port, the centre of all the city's financial and commercial operations.

Standing on a tall plinth and encircled by austere Doric columns, the building is reminiscent of a Greek temple. Its central part is taken up by an enormous top-lighted hall. The sculptured groups, *Neptune with Two Rivers* on the pediment of the east façade and *Navigation with Mercury and Two Rivers* on the attic of the west façade, were carved from Pudost stone by the master stonemason Samson Sukhanov.

Housed here since 1940 is the Central Naval Museum, one of the oldest museums in Russia, which came into being almost simultaneously with the birth of the Russian fleet. Its predecessor was the Ship-model Chamber founded by Peter the Great in 1709 as a repository of models and working drawings of navy vessels. In 1805, the Chamber was reorganized into the Naval Museum.

The Naval Museum was one of the first in the country to open its doors to the public after the October Revolution (February 1918). It has expanded considerably over the years and today boasts over five hundred thousand exhibits which include a priceless collection of ship-models, revolutionary and military relics and various works of art.

52 Museum of Anthropology and Ethnography of the USSR Academy of Sciences (the former *Kunstkammer*)

An early example of Russian architecture in the first third of the 18th century, this building was originally intended to house the first Russian museum, a library, the Academy of Sciences, an anatomy class and an astronomical observatory. It was built between 1718 and 1734 by Nikolaus Herbel, Gaetano Chiaveri, Georg Johann Mattarnovi and Mikhail Zemtsov. In 1747, it was damaged by fire and restored by Sabbas Chevakinsky. The peaked superstructure of the tower, however, was recreated only in the course of restoration work in 1947–48.

The museum's ethnographic collections are devoted to the history, economy, architecture, and artistic handicrafts of the peoples of Asia, Africa, America, and Australia. The Department of Far East contains collections of art works by Chinese, Korean and Viet-Namese craftsmen. A place apart is allotted to the collection brought in by the outstanding Russian scientist and explorer, Miklukho-Maklai, who was a staff member of the museum.

54–56 Equestrian Statue of Peter the Great

The statue of Peter the Great on Decembrists' Square, known as the Bronze Horseman, after Pushkin's poem of the same name, is one of the finest achievements of monumental sculpture. It was created in 1782 by Etienne-Maurice Falconet. Peter's head was executed by Marie-Anne Collot, a pupil of Falconet.

The pedestal of the statue is a granite rock 8 metres high and weighing 1,600 tons.

58, 59 Central Historical Archives (the former Senate and Synod buildings)

These two buildings, which housed the highest ranking arms of government in pre-revolutionary Russia, the Senate and the Synod, are connected by an arch. Built between 1829 and 1834 by Alexander Staubert to the design of Carlo Rossi, they form part of the architectural complex of Decembrists' Square.

The sculptural décor was created by Stepan Pimenov, Vasily Demuth-Malinovsky, Pavel Sokolov, Nikolai Tokarev, and others.

60, 61 The Main Exhibition Hall (the former Horse Guards Manège)

The Horse Guards Manège was built by Giacomo Quarenghi between 1804 and 1807 in the Classical style typical for the late 18th and early 19th century. In plan the building is an elongated rectangle; its interior was formerly a riding-school.

The main façade is decorated with a double-colonnaded portico; the pediment is topped by several statues. On the inside wall of the portico is a low relief depicting equestrian sports. The entrance to the building is flanked with two marble groups representing the Dioscuri modelled by Paolo Triscorni.

In 1967, the building was handed over to the Artists' Union to be used as an exhibition hall.

Two columns topped with the statues of Victory were erected between the Manège and the Synod building. They were conceived by Carlo Rossi who was responsible for the architectural ensemble of this area. The polished columns and pedestals are cut out of monoliths of Serdobol granite. The statues were cast in Berlin after models by Christian Daniel Rauch.

The side façade of the Main Exhibition Hall faces a boulevard laid out where there was once the Admiralty Canal.

62, 65–73, 74 St. Isaac's Square

St. Isaac's Square is one of the largest and most attractive squares in Leningrad.

Besides the St. Isaac Cathedral, the ensemble of the square includes a house built between 1817 and 1820 by Auguste Montferrand for Count Lobanov-Rostovsky. At the far end of the square stands the Mariinsky Palace built in 1839–44 by Andrei Stakenschneider. The building now houses the Executive Committee of the Leningrad City Soviet of People's Deputies.

Nearer the cathedral, and framing the square on two sides, are two similar buildings designed by Nikolai Yefimov for the Ministry of State Property. Both buildings now house the research institutes of the Lenin Academy of Agricultural Sciences.

An equestrian statue of Nicholas I by Piotr Klodt was erected in the centre of the square in the late 1850s.

63, 64 St. Isaac's Cathedral

Designed by Auguste Montferrand and erected between 1818 and 1858, St. Isaac's is one of the most monumental structures in the world of its size, exterior and interior decoration. Many-columned porticos surround the building on all four sides. The monolithic granite columns are 17 metres high and each one weighs 114 tons. The sculptural décor of the edifice consists of about four hundred pieces executed by Ivan Vitali, Piotr Klodt, and Alexander Loganovsky.

The cathedral is surmounted by a tall drum crowned by a gilt dome with an octagonal lantern; four turrets by the sides of the drum serve as bell-towers.

The interior décor of the cathedral is a symphony of gold, marble, lazulite, malachite and porphyry. The walls and vaults are covered with painted and mosaic compositions executed by Karl Briullov, Fiodor Bruni, Piotr Basin, Vasily Shebuyev, and others.

St. Isaac's Cathedral is 101.5 metres high and dominates the central part of the city. Its gilt dome is visible from points dozens of miles away.

In 1931, the cathedral was converted into a museum. Numerous schemes, documents, models, and mock-ups speak of the work performed by the talented and ingenious architects, engineers, stonemasons, and founders who erected this magnificent edifice, and of the back-breaking toil by scores of thousands of serfs that the project entailed.

75, 76 The Executive Committee of the Leningrad City Soviet of People's Deputies (the former Mariinsky Palace)

The Mariinsky Palace was built by Andrei Stakenschneider between 1839 and 1844. The central part of the building is adorned with a massive attic, decorative columns, and a wide balcony atop an arcaded porch. The palace has a sumptuous interior décor. The suite of state rooms does not run parallel to the main façade but leads into the depths of the building along its central axis. This is the only example in 19th-century Russian architecture of a palace suite being so laid out.

On October 25 (November 7, New Style), 1917, the palace was occupied by units of the Military Revolutionary Committee. A meeting of the Bureau of the Supreme Economic Council held here in December 1917 was attended by Lenin.

From 1945 this building has been the seat of the Executive Committee of the Leningrad City Soviet of People's Deputies. Flying above the roof is the flag of the Russian Federation, and on the attic are represented the State Emblem of the Federation and the government decorations awarded to Leningrad.

77, 78 The former Admiralty

This magnificent building, one of the supreme achievements of Russian Classicism, is the architectural and compositional pivot of the city. Its present-day look took about a hundred years to achieve. Construction of the first Admiralty (a fortified shipyard) was begun in 1704. The second was designed by Ivan Korobov and erected between 1727 and 1738. The now existing Admiralty building was put up in 1806–23 to the design of Adrian Zakharov.

In the latter half of the 19th century the territory of the former shipyard was taken up by residential buildings which shut the Admiralty off from the Neva embankment. Access to the Neva is through the archways of two symmetrically situated pavilions.

The main façade runs parallel to Admiralty Prospekt; in the centre of the building is a graceful tower topped by a gilt spire (72.5 metres high overall) with a weather-vane in the shape of a caravel on its tip. The central and side façades are decorated with multi-columned porticos.

An integral part of the Admiralty's architecture is its sculptured décor which accentuates the building's *raison d'être*—navigation and shipbuilding. The central relief on the attic is entitled *The Establishment of a Fleet in Russia* (by Ivan Terebeniov). Flanking the central arch are two sculptural groups of sea nymphs supporting the Earth's sphere. On the top corners of the tower's lower cube are four statues of classical heroes and military leaders—Achilles, Ajax, Pyrrhus and Alexander the Great (by Theodosius Shchedrin). The columns of the upper cube are surmounted by statues personifying the four elements—fire, water, air, and earth; the four seasons of the year—spring, summer, autumn, and winter; and the four winds—south, west, north, and east. Also placed here are the figures of Isis, the patroness of seafaring, and Urania, the Muse of astronomy (by Stepan Pimenov and Shchedrin). The low reliefs adorning the four porticos were executed by Terebeniov.

79, 82, 83 The former General Staff building

Designed by Carlo Rossi, this building was erected between 1819 and 1829 to house the General Staff and two government ministries—finance and foreign affairs. The imposing edifice with its semicircle of curvilinear blocks fronts a large square before the Winter Palace. In the centre of the almost six-hundred-metre-long façade is a triumphal arch, a monument to Russia's victory over Napoleon in the War of 1812–14. The sides of the archway are ornamented with trophies, and there are figures of warriors between its columns. Crowning the arch is the winged figure of Victory driving a six-horse chariot. The authors of these sculptures were Stepan Pimenov and Vasily Demuth-Malinovsky.

80, 81 Palace Square

Palace Square is extremely rich in historical associations.

On January 9 (January 22, New Style), 1905, processions of workers came here carrying a petition to the Tsar. But the Tsar's soldiers opened fire, and hundreds of people were killed or wounded. That day known as Bloody Sunday marked the beginning of the first Russian revolution.

On October 25 (November 7, New Style), 1917, the revolutionary Red Guards rushed across the square, broke through the fortifications and seized the Winter Palace, the seat of the Provisional Government. The Socialist Revolution won.

Now the square serves as a parade ground during the celebration of state and revolutionary holidays.

84–125 The Hermitage (the former Winter Palace)

The Winter Palace was designed by Bartolommeo Rastrelli and built between 1754 and 1762 as a winter residence for the reigning monarch. Thousands of labourers and artisans took part in its construction.

One of Rastrelli's finest creations, the Winter Palace is a typical Baroque structure. Its magnificent architecture and sumptuous sculptural ornamentation make it the dominant feature of the city's centre. West to east the building is about 230 metres long. All the palace's façades are lavishly decorated. The projecting parts of the walls are adorned with columns, and the corners of the buildings with clusters of columns.

The south façade overlooking Palace Square has three archways that open into an extensive courtyard. The main entrance is in the north façade of the palace, from the side of the Neva, and leads directly to the Jordan Staircase.

After 1762 the interior of the palace was redesigned several times. In 1837, all its interior decoration was destroyed by fire. The present interior décor was executed in 1838–39 from the designs of Vasily Stasov and Alexander Briullov. They recreated, with only minor alterations, the Small Throne Hall, the Main (Jordan) Staircase and the 1812 Gallery. The façades of the buildings were restored to their original aspect.

After the February revolution that overthrew the tsarist régime, the palace was for a short time the seat of the counter-revolutionary Provisional Government. On the night of October 25 (November 7, New Style), 1917, the Winter Palace was taken by storm by revolutionary workers, soldiers and sailors, and it was here that the Provisional Government was deposed.

Today the Winter Palace is one of the buildings that make up the Hermitage, the fabulously rich treasure-house of art and culture whose collections enjoy world renown. The first large consignment of pictures arrived at the Winter Palace in 1764, and it is from this date that the Hermitage counts its beginnings.

The Hermitage Museum occupies five buildings: the Winter Palace, the Small Hermitage designed by Jean-Baptiste Vallin de la Mothe (1764–75), the Old Hermitage by Yury Velten (1771–87), the Hermitage Theatre by Giacomo Quarenghi (1783–87) and the New Hermitage by Vasily Stasov and Nikolai Yefimov from a design of Leo von Klenze (1839–52).

The museum's oldest department is that of Western European art. Among the great names represented are Leonardo da Vinci, Raphael, Giorgione, Rembrandt, and others. It also has a valuable collection of French art. The Department of Antique Art boasts a priceless collection of ancient sculpture and archaeological relics, which is constantly being enlarged by new finds from expeditions conducted by the Hermitage and the USSR Academy of Sciences.

Visitors to the Department of Russian Culture may also take in the October Doorway through which those storming the Winter Palace burst into its premises, as well as the Malachite Room and the White Dining-room where the ministers of the deposed Provisional Government were arrested.

135 The Alexander Column

This column, built in 1829–34 from a design by Auguste Montferrand, was put up in the centre of Palace Square to commemorate Russia's victory over Napoleon in the War of 1812–14.

The pedestal of the column is adorned with bronze compositions in relief executed by P. Svintsov, I. Leppe and S. Balin after drawings by Montferrand and Giovanni Battista Scotti. The column is crowned by the figure of an angel holding a cross in one hand, the work of Boris Orlovsky.

The column was hewn out of a dark-red granite monolith under the supervision of the talented stonemason Yakovlev. It is kept secure on the pedestal entirely by its own weight.

The overall height of the monument is 47.5 metres.

136 The Winter Canal

This little canal connects the Neva with the Moika. It got its name from an earlier Winter Palace, built here in the 18th century for Peter the Great and later replaced by the Hermitage Theatre. The canal was dug in 1718–20. It is spanned by three bridges—the First Winter Bridge, the Second Winter Bridge and the Hermitage Bridge, all put up in the 18th century.

139, 140 The Pushkin Memorial Museum

The museum, a branch of the All-Union Pushkin Museum, is situated in the apartment where the great Russian poet resided from October 1836 to the day of his death, January 29 (February 10, New Style), 1837.

All the furnishings of the apartment where the poet lived his last months have been recreated from archival documents. Some of Pushkin's personal belongings are housed here, as well as several artifacts of his time.

The museum consists of ten rooms. One of them is a study. Here Pushkin worked on *The History of Peter the Great*, wrote articles for the literary journal *The Contemporary* and completed his tale *The Captain's Daughter*. Here he would receive visiting friends, mostly writers and poets, and it is here that he died. The hands of a Gothic clock point to the moment of the poet's passing—2:45 p.m.

141–156 The Summer Gardens and the Summer Palace of Peter the Great

The Summer Gardens and the Summer Palace of Peter the Great are magnificent examples of early 18th-century Russian architecture and landscape gardening. The Gardens were laid out in 1704 in the formal style by Matveyev, Zemtsov, Jan Roosen, Surmin, Lukyanov, and others. Many of the elements that go to make a formal garden have not come down to our day, but the geometric lay-out of the Gardens' avenues and walks and their unique collection of marble statuary by early 18th-century Italian masters have been preserved intact.

From the Neva side the Gardens are bordered by railings of magnificent ironwork, designed by Yury Velten. The strict forms of the railings and their clear-cut composition put them on a par with the finest works of Russian Classicism.

The pavilions, arbours, fountains, and other ornamental structures of the Gardens were destroyed by flood in 1777 and were never rebuilt. The existing Coffee- and Tea-houses were constructed by Louis Charlemagne and Carlo Rossi only in the 19th century.

Installed here in 1855 was a monument by Piotr Klodt to Krylov, the eminent Russian fabulist.

The Summer Gardens rank among the most popular pleasure grounds of the city.

Peter the Great's Summer Palace was the monarch's state residence in St. Petersburg. It was built between 1710 and 1712 to the design of Domenico Trezzini. The two-storey structure with a hipped roof is adorned with a frieze and low-relief compositions glorifying in allegorical form Russia's victories in the Great Northern War. Some of the rooms retain elements of their original decoration—tiled walls, carved panels, and stucco mouldings. Of particular interest are Peter's Study, the Green Room, the Presence Room, and some others. The Summer Palace was transformed into a museum in 1934. On permanent display in its rooms are works of fine and applied art, furniture and utility items characteristic of palace interiors in the first quarter of the 18th century.

158 The Pavilion in the Mikhailovsky Garden

Built in 1825 by Carlo Rossi, this little garden pavilion-cum-pier is noteworthy for its elegant proportions and beautiful details. The painted ceiling inside the Pavilion has been preserved intact. The granite terrace on the Moika bank is surrounded by a cast-iron fence executed after a drawing by Rossi.

159 Malokoniushenny and Theatre Bridges

Designed by Yegor Adam and Georges Traitteur and built in 1829–31, the bridges constitute an interesting ensemble, the only one of its kind in the world. Theatre Bridge spanning the Moika River is positioned dead along the axis of the Catherine (now Griboyedov) Canal, and leading up to it from both banks of the canal are two drives which make up Malokoniushenny Bridge. The whole ensemble was referred to in those days as the "triple arch" bridge. The façade arches of the bridges are richly ornamented, their cast-iron railings are adorned with masks and palmettes.

160–162 The Engineers' (Mikhailovsky) Castle

An outstanding monument of late 18th-century Russian architecture, the castle was designed by Vasily Bazhenov and built between 1797 and 1800 by Vincenzo Brenna as a sort of fortified residence. The main (south) façade is impressive in its solemn grandeur. Its central portion is faced with marble and decorated with two obelisks, an attic, and a colonnade supporting a triangular pediment with a low-relief composition. Equally imposing is the north façade overlooking the Summer Gardens: the attic here is embellished with caryatids and low reliefs executed by Paolo Triscorni and Philippe Thiébot. The side projections are linked by a Doric colonnade which is surmounted by a balcony. The broad staircase is adorned with statues of Flora and Hercules. The castle used to be surrounded by a moat with drawbridges; later the moat was filled in.

In 1823, the castle was given over to the School of Military Engineers (hence the name Engineers' Castle). Among its graduates over the years were Dostoyevsky, Kondratenko, a hero of the Russo-Japanese War, and the fortifications engineer Karbyshev, Hero of the Soviet Union.

Only the main staircase, the Throne Hall, the Raphael Gallery, the Oval and Church Halls have partially preserved their décor.

In 1800, an equestrian statue of Peter the Great by Carlo Rastrelli was put up in front of the palace.

The Engineers' Castle ensemble also includes two pavilions facing Engineers' Street and the building of the former riding school (now the Winter Stadium) with its stables.

163, 165–183 The Russian Museum (the former Mikhailovsky Palace)

The palace was built by Carlo Rossi between 1819 and 1825. Its central part stands back from the square and faces the front courtyard formed by the two side pavilions and the monumental cast-iron railing. The stately aspect of the main façade stems largely from its Corinthian colonnade. The relief compositions were executed by Vasily Demuth-Malinovsky and Stepan Pimenov, who also took part in the interior decoration of the palace.

The palace, which is the compositional pivot of the architectural ensemble on Arts Square, presents an impressive picture, culminating the vista from Nevsky Prospect down Brodsky Street. The façade overlooking the Mikhailovsky Garden is in the form of a broad loggia. In 1896–97, Vasily Svinyin reconstructed some of the palace's interiors to adapt it for use as a museum of Russian art. A number of interiors, however, were left unaltered and retain their original décor to this day (the vestibule, the grand staircase, the White Hall, and others).

At present the palace building houses the Russian Museum which is one of the country's largest depositories of Russian national art.

The museum was founded in 1895. After the October Revolution its collections increased severalfold. A department of Soviet art was organized.

The museum occupies two buildings—the former Mikhailovsky Palace and an adjacent building facing the Griboyedov Canal Embankment, erected in 1912–17 by Leonty Benois and Sergei Ovsiannikov.

The Department of Old Russian Art (9th–17th centuries) is devoted to works by masters of the Novgorod, Moscow, and Pskov schools of painting.

The sections displaying the art of the 18th and first half of the 19th centuries are unmatched for the scope and variety of their exhibits. Represented are such artists as Rokotov, Levitsky, Borovikovsky, Briullov, Kiprensky, Ivanov, Venetsianov, Fedotov, Shubin, Shchedrin, Gordeyev, Kozlovsky, and Martos.

A separate exhibition illustrates the art of the second half of the 19th century with works by Repin, Surikov, Levitan, Perov, Kramskoi, Savrasov, Shishkin, Polenov, Makovsky, and Vasnetsov.

Canvases by Russian artists of the late 19th and early 20th centuries vividly reflect the struggle then being fought between the various schools and trends of Russian art. On display here are pictures by Serov, Arkhipov, Kasatkin, Korovin, Roerich, Dobuzhinsky, and Kustodiev.

The works of Soviet painters, Rylov, Petrov-Vodkin, Nesterov, Sergei Gerasimov, Deineka, Plastov, Mylnikov, Moiseyenko, Korzhev, and others, testify to the inseparable links of their art with the life around them.

164 Statue of Pushkin on Arts Square

The statue of Pushkin by Mikhail Anikushin, one of the best monuments to the great Russian poet in Leningrad, was unveiled in June 1957. The pedestal of polished red granite was designed by Vasily Petrov. The statue blends admirably with the ensemble.

184, 187 The Museum of the Ethnography of the Peoples of the USSR

The building was designed by Vasily Svinyin who made generous use of the architectural devices and motifs of Russian Classicism to achieve stylistic integration with the Mikhailovsky Palace (now the Russian Museum). Linked as it is with the architectural ensemble of the palace, it is nevertheless an original and independent building. Its construction began in the spring of 1900 and was completed in 1911.

During the War of 1941–45 bombing attacks and artillery fire caused considerable damage to the building. After the war it was completely restored.

185, 186 The Academic Maly Theatre of Opera and Ballet (the former Mikhailovsky Theatre)

The interior of the theatre was designed by Alexander Briullov. The cornerstone of the building was laid in August 1831; the theatre was opened in November 1833.

The exterior of the building does not differ much from that of the near-by houses designed by Carlo Rossi, who had planned the ensemble of the entire square. In 1859–60 the theatre was reconstructed by Albert Cavos.

In 1918, the building was given over to the Maly Theatre of Opera and Ballet. Its company is known for a number of successful productions of world-famous operas and ballets.

In 1950–51 the auditorium of the theatre was renovated and the building was partially reconstructed.

188 Grand Concert Hall of the Leningrad Philharmonic Society

The Leningrad Philharmonic Society building was erected between 1834 and 1839 by Paul Jacquot, who also designed its grand concert hall famous for its superb acoustics.

The hall is decorated by columns of the Corinthian order faced with white imitation marble. The side walls with broad arches resting on Ionic columns are adorned by pilasters.

The central part of the hall is surrounded by two-tiered galleries. In 1931, the hall was altered to increase its seating capacity.

On August 9, 1942, the Seventh Symphony of Dmitry Shostakovich, composed in the besieged Leningrad and dedicated to the heroic city, was performed in the Grand Hall of the Philharmonic, only 13 kilometres from the front line. It was conducted by Karl Eliasberg and played by the veterans of the orchestra of the Leningrad Radio Centre, many of the musicians wearing military uniform. The symphony was broadcast by all the radio stations in the Soviet Union to many countries and produced a tremendous impression on the world public.

189, 190 The former Stroganov Palace

The Stroganov Palace was built in 1752–54 by Bartolommeo Rastrelli. Its Nevsky Prospekt façade is decorated with columns resting on rusticated pedestals and with sculptural details in the form of leonine masks, caryatids, and figures of cupids. The spacious hall with windows arranged in two tiers and with a ceiling painted by Giuseppe Valeriani has been preserved unaltered from Rastrelli's time.

In the first half of the 1790s, the palace was rebuilt by Andrei Voronikhin; the interiors were redecorated in the Classical style. The Mineral, Arabesque, and Corner Rooms deserve special interest as significant artistic achievements.

After completion of ongoing restoration work the building will house a branch of the Russian Museum.

195 The former Catholic Church of St. Catherine

The original design of the Catholic church belonged to P. Trezzini, who suggested to set it farther back from the road and to build two identical three-storey apartment houses on either side. The houses were eventually erected to his design, but the church itself was built by Vallin de la Mothe (the project was approved on May 9, 1762). For some years the construction works were supervised by Antonio Rinaldi.

The portal of the main façade of the church is an arch supported by two columns. The parapet of the attic carries the sculptures of the Four Evangelists and two angels with a cross in the centre.

202 Statue of Kutuzov

This monument to the famous Russian military leader was unveiled on December 25 (January 6, New Style), 1837. The bronze figure of Kutuzov was cast from a model by Boris Orlovsky, the granite pedestal was designed by Vasily Stasov. The symmetrically placed statue of Barclay de Tolly is also by Orlovsky.

202–205 Museum of the History of Religion and Atheism (the former Cathedral of Our Lady of Kazan)

The cathedral, an architectural monument of Russian Classicism, was designed and built between 1801 and 1811 by Andrei Voronikhin. After the War of 1812 the cathedral became a pantheon of Russian military glory: in 1813, the remains of Field Marshal Kutuzov were transferred to the cathedral; captured enemy colours, keys to enemy cities taken by the Russian army in the war against Napoleon, and other war relics were also deposited here. In 1837, monuments to Kutuzov and Barclay de Tolly by Boris Orlovsky were erected in front of the cathedral.

The cathedral is in plan an elongated cross: it is decorated on three sides by porticos of the Corinthian order. The colonnade of its Nevsky Prospekt façade encloses a broad semicircular space. The edifice is surmounted by a light and elegant dome on a tall drum adorned with pilasters. The cathedral stands about 70 metres high. Its facing, pilasters, columns, and elements of its sculptural décor are all done in pale-yellow Pudost stone. The ornamentation of the cathedral was the work of the finest sculptors and painters of the time—Fiodor Gordeyev, Ivan Prokofyev, Ivan Martos, Theodosius Shchedrin, Vasily Shebuyev, and others.

Inside the cathedral are 56 monolithic pillars (each about 11 metres high) of red granite with bases and Corinthian capitals of bronze.

The monumental, beautifully patterned railing forms a small square fronting the west (main) doorway.

The cathedral has served as premises to the USSR Academy of Sciences' Museum of the History of Religion and Atheism since 1932.

211 Monument to Catherine II

The monument was designed in 1862 by Mikhail Mikeshin in cooperation with Matvei Chizhov, who modelled the figure of Catherine II; Alexander Opekushin, who executed the figures of the most distinguished contemporaries of the empress; and David Grimm, who designed the pedestal and supervised the actual construction.

The monument was unveiled in 1873.

211–213 The Pushkin Drama Theatre (the former Alexandrinsky Theatre)

This building, one of the most outstanding architectural monuments of Russian Classicism, was designed by Carlo Rossi and erected between 1828 and 1832. The rusticated walls of the ground storey serve as a plinth for the colonnades decorating the theatre's façades. The colonnade of the main façade, consisting of six Corinthian columns, stands out sharply against the receding wall. The traditional classical portico is replaced here by a loggia, which was rather unusual for St. Petersburg. A major role in the decoration of the façade belongs to sculptures by Stepan Pimenov, Vasily Demuth-Malinovsky, and Alessandro Triscorni. The chariot of Apollo was made out of beaten copper from a model by Pimenov.

No less imposing are the side façades and the south façade which culminates the vista down Rossi Street.

214, 215 The Saltykov-Shchedrin Public Library

The Public Library buildings, though erected at different periods, are an integral part of the ensemble of Ostrovsky Square. The oldest of the three structures which are joined to form a single whole is the building whose façades overlook Sadovaya Street, Nevsky Prospekt, and Ostrovsky Square—it was put up between 1796 and 1801 by Yegor Sokolov. The rusticated ground storey is transpierced by semicircular and rectangular window apertures which create the impression of an arcade. It serves as a socle for a colonnade of the Ionic order. In 1828–34, a new building, designed by Carlo Rossi, was appended to the old one. Rossi used the architectural motifs of the first library building for its façades—arched shallow niches for the ground storey, and the Ionic order for the colonnade. Statues of ancient scientists, philosophers, and poets were placed between the columns. These figures were sculpted by Stepan Pimenov, Vasily Demuth-Malinovsky, Samuel Galberg, Nikolai Tokarev, and Mikhail Krylov. The low reliefs and the statue of Minerva crowning the attic of the main façade were executed by Demuth-Malinovsky.

Between 1896 and 1901 Yevgraf Vorotilov erected a spacious building to house a reading-hall, linking it into a single whole with the building put up by Rossi.

The library as such was founded in 1795 and opened to readers in 1814. It served as the central state library and was the first public library in Russia. Beginning with 1810 it received two copies of every printed work published in the country.

In 1893–95, Lenin spent much time working in the library's reading-hall. After the October Revolution he took a sympathetic interest in its activities and saw to the adequate replenishment of its stocks. It was on Lenin's initiative that a number of valuable collections of books in Petrograd were handed over to the library, a measure that guaranteed their preservation and their accessibility to a wide circle of readers.

The Public Library became truly public only in the Soviet years of its existence.

The library did not cease to function, if only for a day, even in the impossible conditions of the siege of Leningrad during the War of 1941–45.

In the Soviet years the library's stocks have increased immensely. They now number over 17 million inventory units. These include literature in 89 languages of the peoples of the USSR, in all the European languages and in 156 Oriental and African languages. Among the library's most treasured possessions are its collections of Russian manuscript and printed books, the most complete in the country; works by Marx, Engels, and Lenin published in their lifetime; manuscripts by many outstanding figures of Russian and foreign culture. The foreign section includes the library of Voltaire, documents relating to the French Revolution of 1789–94, the archives of the Bastille, and publications of the Paris Commune period.

The library is second in the country for the wealth of its stocks (the first being the Lenin Library in Moscow) and one of the largest in the world.

216 Kuibyshevsky District Committee of the CPSU (the former Palace of the Counts Beloselsky-Belozersky)

The palace was designed in 1846 by Andrei Stakenschneider, who followed 18th-century examples of the Russian Baroque style in architecture, such as the Stroganov Palace and the Sheremetev Palace.

The building is decorated with colonnaded porticos, window platbands of intricate pattern, and atlantes modelled by D. Jenssen.

The interiors of the palace were restored in 1954. The broad flights of the main staircase are provided with fine openwork railings. Statues supporting candelabra are placed symmetrically in niches.

The walls of the library are lined with silk in the upper part and with gilt wood panels in the lower part.

217 The Palace of Young Pioneers (the former Anichkov Palace)

Construction of the palace was begun in 1741 by Mikhail Zemtsov. After his death it was continued from 1743 by Grigory Dmitriyev, who altered the original design. Built in the style of Russian Baroque, the palace had its main façade overlooking the Fontanka River. In the centre of the gallery-encircled courtyard was a pool connected with the river by a canal. Owing to alterations made by Ivan Starov, Luigi Rusca, Carlo Rossi, and Maximilian Messmacher the building lost its Baroque character.

From 1918 to 1935 the palace housed the Museum of the History of Leningrad. In 1935–37, it was reconstructed by Alexander Gegello and David Krichevsky and began to function as the Palace of Young Pioneers. Among those who participated in its interior decoration were folk painters from Palekh.

218, 219 Anichkov Bridge

This three-span masonry bridge over the Fontanka is one of the most beautiful in Leningrad. It was built in 1839–41 by Andrei Gotman. The cast-iron railings are from a drawing by Karl Friedrich Schinkel.

The bridge is adorned with four sculptured groups, each representing a youth holding a horse in check and symbolizing man's struggle with the wild, uncontrollable forces of nature. These sculptures, by Piotr Klodt, must be viewed counter-clockwise, beginning with the one nearest the Palace of Young Pioneers.

221, 226, 228 Lomonosov (Chernyshov) Bridge

Built in 1785–87 by A. Viazemsky, this three-span bridge was similar in design to the stone bridges that then spanned the Fontanka. Granite towers topped by domes were erected on the piers of the bridge, and placed inside them were special mechanisms for raising the central span to allow the passage of sailing vessels. Because of a heavy increase in city traffic by the mid-19th century the bascule bridges over the Fontanka were reconstructed: the turrets were pulled down and the machinery for manipulating the bascule was removed. In that respect Lomonosov Bridge was least affected: in 1912, it was rebuilt into a cantilever bridge on metal beams, but its turrets remained intact. The granite obelisks with lanterns and figured corbels were restored in 1950.

222, 225 The former Sheremetev Palace

The Sheremetev Palace was built in 1750–55 by Sabbas Chevakinsky and Fiodor Argunov. Compositionally this is a typical manor house with an inner courtyard and a garden at the back. The manor grounds are fenced off from the Fontanka Embankment by a cast-iron railing (architect Geronimo Corsini, late 1830s).

The decoration of the façades is a blend of traditional Petrine elements with moulded window platbands, leonine masks, and elaborate capitals characteristic of the Baroque style.

229, 232, 233 The House of Friendship and Peace (the former Shuvalov Palace)

Built in the 1820s by an anonymous architect, the palace was reconstructed in the 1840s by Bernard Simon who redecorated all the interiors except the Columned Hall, with its bas-relief panel on Trojan War themes and ceiling painting by Giovanni Battista Scotti. Deserving of interest are the entrance hall, the grand staircase with colonnades on the first floor, the Mauve, Blue and Gilt Drawing-rooms, and the Knights' Hall with its relief representations of tournaments. Destroyed during the War of 1941–45, the palace was restored by Mikhail Plotnikov in the 1960s.

Housed in the palace since 1965 is the Leningrad Section of the Union of Soviet Friendship Societies, which acquaints Leningraders with the culture of foreign countries and popularizes abroad the achievements of Leningrad in the fields of science and culture.

234 Bank Bridge

This is one of the six suspension bridges over the Griboyedov Canal erected in St. Petersburg in the first quarter of the 19th century. These bridges were the first of their type in Europe.

Bank Bridge over the Griboyedov Canal was built in 1825–26 by Georges Traitteur. The cast-iron abutments securing the cables by which the span of the bridge is anchored are embedded in the masonry of the embankment and hidden from view by cast-iron figures of fantastic gryphons modelled by Pavel Sokolov. The bridge has elegantly patterned railings. The wings of the gryphons and the tops of the lanterns are covered with gilding.

245 The Dostoyevsky Memorial Museum

The museum was opened in 1971 to mark the 150th anniversary of the famous novelist's birth. Dostoyevsky lived in a flat here for the last four years of his life, from 1878 to 1881.

The museum includes the memorial flat and an exposition reflecting Dostoyevsky's work.

The writer's flat has been painstakingly recreated to its original appearance.

The exposition includes materials connected with the creation of the novels which became landmarks in the history of Russian and world literature: *Crime and Punishment*, *The Gambler*, *The Idiot*, *The Possessed*, *Brothers Karamazov*, etc. Also on display are photographs and letters of the novelist and his relatives, his manuscripts and notes, as well as drawings and illustrations for his books.

246 Apartment House on the Fontanka Embankment

Erected in 1910–12 by Fiodor Lidval, it is typical of housing construction in St. Petersburg in the early 20th century, when the cost of land, especially in the centre of the city, kept going up. The architects were compelled to build the multi-storey apartment houses close together on a rectangular plan, with narrow courtyards resembling wells.

This house has three courtyards connected by three-storey-high archways with lanterns of forged iron suspended from their vaults.

Unlike most of the apartment houses built in St. Petersburg in the 19th century, the façades of the house, including those overlooking the courtyards, are decorated.

The Renaissance motifs of the archways are beautifully combined with oval windows, intricate moulded stucco decorations, and unplastered brick characteristic of the Art Nouveau style.

248 The Blok Memorial Museum

The museum was opened in November 1980 to mark the 100th anniversary of Alexander Blok's birth. From 1912 to 1921, the poet lived at No. 57 in Decembrists' Street. His most significant poems, *The Nightingale Garden*, *Retribution*, *The Twelve*, as well as revolutionary articles of 1918–21 and the play *The Rose and the Cross*, were written in this house.

In one of the two memorial flats constituting the museum the poet lived till 1920. The study, dining-room, bedroom and drawing-room in this flat have been restored according to pictures, photographs, and reminiscences of those who knew Alexander Blok during his lifetime. The second memorial flat belonged to Blok's mother, and it was here that the poet died on August 7, 1921.

249 Lions' Bridge

Lions' Bridge, one of the six suspension bridges over the Griboyedov Canal, was built in 1825–26 by Georges Traitteur. The powerful figures of the lions modelled by Pavel Sokolov, seated on massive pedestals, are there not only for decorative purposes; they also act as covers for the cast-iron abutments inside them that secure the cables suspending the span of the bridge. The lamp posts rise directly out of the railings.

250, 251 The Kirov Opera and Ballet Theatre (the former Mariinsky Theatre)

The theatre building was designed in 1859 by Albert Cavos. In 1883–96, it was rebuilt by A. Schröter, who reconstructed the façades and interiors and improved the acoustics of the auditorium. Decorating the main façade with a loggia, he made an attempt to lend a classical character to the building. Unfortunately the loggia was swamped by a mass of minute details. The auditorium was built to the multi-tier design common at the time.

The Kirov Opera and Ballet Theatre is one of the oldest theatres in the USSR and enjoys a world reputation. Its role in the development of Russian and Soviet opera and ballet is inestimable.

252 The "New Holland" Arch

The origination of the "New Holland" ensemble is connected with the development of St. Petersburg as a shipbuilding centre on the Baltic Sea. The little island, called "New Holland" in Peter the Great's time, came into being following the digging of the Admiralty and Kriukov Canals. In 1765, Sabbas Chevakinsky built several brick warehouses here for storing timber. The façades of these buildings and the arch over the canal that flows into a pool inside the island were designed by Jean-Baptiste Vallin de la Mothe. The stately "New Holland" arch spanning the canal ranks among the most widely-known architectural monuments of Leningrad. The granite Tuscan columns are strictly classical in their proportions.

254, 255 The Palace of Labour (the former Nikolayevsky Palace)

The Horse Guards Boulevard (now Boulevard Profsoyuzov), laid out in 1844–45, used to connect Senate Square and a newly-created square situated near Annunciation Bridge (later Nikolayevsky Bridge, now Lt. Schmidt Bridge). The bridge was constructed in connection with the building of a new palace for Nicholas I's son, Grand Duke Nicholas. The palace was designed by Andrei Stakenschneider and erected between 1853 and 1861. The façades of the palace have three tiers of pilasters and are adorned by numerous decorative details.

After the October Revolution, on Lenin's initiative, the building was handed over to the trade unions and has been known since as the Palace of Labour.

256–258 The Academy of Art

This building, one of the first examples of Russian Classicism, was put up between 1764 and 1788 by Alexander Kokorinov and Vallin de la Mothe. It is rectangular in plan, with a circular central courtyard and four smaller rectangular ones at the corners. The entrance hall on the ground floor, the main staircase, and the suite of rooms on the first floor are the most imposing features of the interior. They are distinguished by compositional perfection and rich decoration.

The main entrance to the Academy is adorned by a portico with Tuscan columns and a triangular pediment, a motif characteristic of Baroque architecture.

Originally the circular courtyard (about 40 metres in diameter) had access to the Neva embankment through the passage which was in 1817 turned into the present entrance hall, the only part of the building which has preserved its original aspect. The upper entrance hall was partly reconstructed. Now it is decorated with the Ionic colonnade supporting a gallery.

Among the graduates of the Academy are many painters, sculptors, engravers, and architects, who have earned fame for Russian and Soviet art.

The present-day building houses various institutions of the USSR Academy of Art, including its museum and the Repin Institute of Painting, Sculpture and Architecture.

259, 260 The University Embankment

The construction of the granite embankment on the Spit of Vasilyevsky Island (between Palace Bridge and Lt. Schmidt Bridge) was begun in 1804. By 1810 the embankment was faced with granite from the Spit to St. Isaac's Bridge over the Neva (later the bridge was demolished). In 1831, work was carried further, up to the building of the Academy of Art. The construction of this part of the embankment, with the granite landing-stage and two sphinxes in front of the Academy, was supervised by Yegor Adam who built a number of bridges in St. Petersburg.

The two sphinxes carved out of syenite in the 13th century B.C. were discovered during the excavations in Egypt in the 1820s. The sphinxes, their faces bearing a likeness to Pharaoh Amenhotep III (1455–1419 B.C.), had been intended for his funerary temple near Thebes. The sphinxes were bought by the Russian Government and brought to St. Petersburg in the spring of 1832 to be used as a decoration of the landing-stage in front of the Academy of Art building, constructed between 1832 and 1834 after a design by Konstantin Thon.

The sphinxes are placed on granite monoliths flanking the steps down to the Neva. The granite benches with the four gryphons and the symmetrical bronze lampophores cast in 1834 add to the beauty of the landing-stage.

261   Statue of Admiral Krusenstern on the Neva Embankment (Vasilyevsky Island)

The bronze figure of the first Russian circumnavigator of the globe was cast from a model by Ivan Schroeder. The pedestal of polished red granite, designed by Hippolyte Monighetti, bears representations of an African and a Malayan personifying the countries explored by Krusenstern.

The statue was put up between 1870 and 1873.

262   The Mining Institute

The building, a remarkable example of the Classical style, was erected between 1806 and 1811 by Andrei Voronikhin to house the first technical school in Russia, later renamed the Mining Institute, whose premises it has remained for over a century and a half.

The main façade is decorated with an imposing dodecastyle portico. The broad stairway is flanked with two sculptured groups: *Heracles and Anteus* by Stepan Pimenov and *Pluto Carrying Off Proserpina* by Vasily Demuth-Malinovsky. On the frieze of the building, on either side of the portico, are two bas-reliefs by Demuth-Malinovsky: *Venus Comes to Vulcan for Mars's Armour* and *Apollo Comes to Claim the Chariot Made for Him by Vulcan*.

The only surviving elements of Voronikhin's original design are the Grand Staircase and the Hall of Columns whose ceiling was painted by Giovanni Battista Scotti.

264   Institute of Russian Literature (known as Pushkin House) of the USSR Academy of Sciences (the former Customs House)

This building, designed by Giovanni Luchini and erected in 1829–32, is part of the architectural complex of the Vasilyevsky Island Spit. The main façade is decorated with an Ionic octastyle portico. The columns rest on the projecting part of the ground floor executed in the manner of a socle. On the pediment of the portico are statues of Mercury, Neptune and Ceres cast in copper. In 1927, the building was assigned to the Institute of

Russian Literature. Exhibits of the institute's museum are on display in the halls of the second floor. The library of the institute houses one of the country's richest collections of Russian literature and literary criticism. Also kept here are Pushkin's manuscripts and his library.

266   The Rumiantsev Obelisk

There is a small garden next to the Academy of Art on the bank of the Neva, and in the middle of it stands a tall granite obelisk, designed by Vincenzo Brenna in honour of the victories scored by Field Marshal Rumiantsev. Originally, in 1799, it stood on the Field of Mars; later it was placed near the Marble Palace; and still later, in 1818, to its present place, between the Academy of Art and the First Cadet Corps where Rumiantsev had received his military training.

The grey marble pedestal of the memorial is decorated with white marble bas-reliefs representing trophies, and with bronze wreaths and garlands. The obelisk is crowned by an eagle on a bronze sphere. The inscription on the pedestal reads: *To Rumiantsev's Victories*.

The Rumiantsev Obelisk is a fine example of the style of Russian Classicism. It determined the lay-out of the garden around it, fenced off by wrought-iron railings. The garden was designed by N. Kovrigin in 1866–67.

268, 270   Leningrad University (the former Twelve Collegia building)

This terrace of twelve pavilion-like buildings is a splendid example of civic architecture in the first third of the 18th century. It was built between 1722 and 1742 by Domenico Trezzini to house Russia's supreme government ministries—the Senate and the *collegia* instituted by Peter the Great. Each building was under its own roof and had its own entrance.

In 1819, the entire *collegia* complex was assigned to the university. This called for certain alterations, which were effected by Apollon Shchedrin.

St. Petersburg University made a significant contribution to the development of Russian science and played a major role in the revolutionary movement of the late 19th and early 20th centuries. It was the Alma Mater of many illustrious figures in the country's sciences and arts— Mechnikov, Pavlov, Mendeleyev, Chernyshevsky, Blok, and others. Lenin's elder brother, Alexander Ulyanov, executed by the tsarist government in 1887, studied here, and Lenin himself sat for his examinations here after completing an extra-mural course in law.

271–273   Branch of the Hermitage (the former Menshikov Palace)

The palace was built for Alexander Menshikov, companion and adviser of Peter the Great, as part of a spacious estate, between 1710 and 1727 by Domenico Fontana and Gottfried Schädel. It far exceeded in size and splendour all St. Petersburg buildings of the time. Each storey of the façade is adorned with pilasters. There used to be an attic over the central part of the palace which was surmounted by sculptures. In spite of numerous alterations effected in the course of the 18th century, the palace has on the whole retained its original aspect. The interior decoration of some of the halls on the first floor—tiles on the walls, tiled stoves, as well as a

painted ceiling and carved wooden panels with inlaid designs in Menshikov's study—has also been preserved inviolate. Now the palace houses a branch of the Hermitage—the Department of Russian Applied Art.

277   Hotel Leningrad

The hotel was designed by S. Speransky, N. Kamensky and V. Struzman with the participation of V. Volonsevich, S. Mikhailov, Ye. Izrailev, and M. Schechner. It was completed in 1970 and is well integrated with the architectural environment. The laconic elongated edifice complies with the main principle governing construction along the banks of the Neva—linear extent. The ramps leading to raised parking platforms naturally connect the embankment with the modern-looking edifice resting on a lowered plinth. The restaurant, which can cater to 1,300 people, is a separate cylindrical structure, and there is a café on the top floor of the hotel. There is also an all-purpose auditorium with seats for 800.

The architects and builders of the hotel were awarded the State Prize of 1973.

278, 279   The Oktiabrsky Concert Hall

This is one of the largest concert halls in Leningrad (4,000 seats). It was inaugurated in 1967 in honour of the 50th anniversary of the October Revolution. The building was designed by V. Kamensky and A. Zhuk, the frieze on its façade was executed by Mikhail Anikushin.

The stage is serviced with sound-amplifying and sound-recording equipment, as well as with a wired radio system for simultaneous translation from foreign languages.

Installed in front of the building is the sculptural group *October* by A. Matveyev.

280, 283   "The Hut" Memorial in Razliv

In July and August 1917 Lenin spent over a month in a hut on the shore of Lake Razliv to escape persecution by the counter-revolutionary Provisional Government. An inscription on the memorial thus records the event: "At this spot, where in July and August of 1917, in a hut built of branches, the leader of the World Revolution took shelter from the persecution of the bourgeoisie and wrote his book *The State and Revolution*, in memory of those events, we have erected this hut of granite. The workers of the city of Lenin. 1927."

Next to this granite monument is a pavilion of granite, marble and glass which was built in 1964 from a design by V. Kirkhoglani, V. Norin, and V. Kondratyev. The exhibits displayed here witness to the huge amount of work done by Lenin during his underground period. From Razliv he presided over the proceedings of the Sixth Congress of the Russian Social Democratic Workers' Party (of Bolsheviks) which oriented the party toward armed uprising.

281   Steam Locomotive No. 293

An old-fashioned steam locomotive No. 293 was installed on the east platform of Finland Railway Station in 1961. Aboard the locomotive Lenin secretly crossed the Russo-Finnish border twice, in August and October 1917.

The locomotive was handed over to the Soviet government as a gift by the government of Finland in 1957.

284 Monument to Lenin in front of Finland Station

This monument ranks among the most significant achievements of Soviet art. It reflects a crucial moment in the history of revolutionary Russia—Lenin's return to Petrograd from abroad on April 3 (16, New Style), 1917, and his speech before thousands of workers, soldiers, and sailors, in which he called on the masses to strive for a socialist revolution.

The monument was designed by Sergei Yevseyev (architects Vladimir Shchuko and Vladimir Helfreich). It was unveiled on November 7, 1926. In 1945–46 it was moved closer to the Neva and became the compositional centre of a newly-created square.

285, 286 The former Bezborodko villa

The central building with its towers was put up in 1773–77 by Vasily Bazhenov, the side pavilions and galleries in 1783–84 by Giacomo Quarenghi, who also partially altered the façades of the main portion. The pavilions are connected by a railing with the fence posts in the form of cast-iron seated lions holding chains. There is an attractive granite landing-stage on the Neva embankment fronting the building.

287 Apartment House on Leo Tolstoy Square

The house was built between 1913 and 1917. The construction was begun by K. Rosenstein and completed by A. Belogrud. Taking as a model a medieval English castle with numerous turrets, Belogrud created an original composition. He paid special attention to the decoration of the façade, a feature typical for the first decade of the 20th century. The outlines of the window openings, the form of the platbands embellished with sculptural decoration, the colouring of the façades—sandstone colour for the walls and brown for the details—are the most noteworthy features of the house.

291 Monument to the Heroic Sailors of the Destroyer *Steregushchy*

The monument, erected in memory of the heroism shown by the sailors of the *Steregushchy*, stands in Kirovsky Prospekt. Heavily damaged in a battle during the Russo-Japanese War of 1904–5, the destroyer was surrounded by enemy warships. Two sailors still alive opened the cocks and went down with their ship preferring to die rather than see it fall into enemy hands. Designed by the sculptor Konstantin Isenberg, the monument was unveiled in 1911.

293 Apartment house on the Karpovka Embankment

Erected in 1931–35 after a design by Yevgeny Levinson and Igor Fomin, the building is beautifully integrated with its setting. Placed on the bank of the winding Karpovka River, the house was to have culminated a projected new street. The configuration of the plot of ground on which it was put up was rather irregular, and this determined the unusual shape of the structure.

294 The Yubileiny Sports Palace

The largest Leningrad auditorium and sports hall with a seating capacity of 8,500, it was opened to the public in 1967, the year of the 50th anniversary of Soviet power.

The authors of the project are G. Morozov, I. Suslikov, A. Levkhanian, F. Yakovlev, A. Morozov, L. Moskaliov, Yu. Yeliseyev, and N. Pukach.

295 Statue of Maxim Gorky

Maxim Gorky, the great Russian writer whose works are remarkable for their realistic power, is rightfully regarded as the founder of socialist realism in literature.

This statue was unveiled in 1968. It was cast in bronze after the model by Vera Isayeva and Mikhail Gabe.

296 The Palace of Youth

The Palace of Youth designed by P. Prokhorov, V. Tropin, A. Izoitko, and V. Pershin was built in 1970. Situated in the western part of Aptekarsky Island, at the end of Professor Popov Street, the palace was intended for events like youth congresses, friendly talks and discussions, athletic competitions, and young people's parties.

In view of the various functions of the palace the architects created a composition based on combining two prism-shaped structures—the vertical one which houses the hotel and the horizontal one comprising a spacious entrance hall, café, winter garden, auditorium, dancing hall, gymnasium, and swimming pool.

298 Statue of Pushkin in the underground hall of the Chornaya Rechka Metro Station

The statue modelled by Mikhail Anikushin was unveiled on February 10, 1983. It was installed in the metro station near the site of Pushkin's duel.

299 Obelisk on the site of Pushkin's duel

On a small clearing near the Chornaya Rechka the great Russian poet was mortally wounded in a duel on January 27 (February 8, New Style), 1837. Surrounded by poplars and willows, the site of the duel is marked by a 19 metre obelisk designed by M. Manizer and A. Lapirov and erected in 1937. The obelisk is made of pink granite with a bronze bas-relief portrait of Pushkin.

300, 301 The Yelagin Palace

Built between 1818 and 1822 by Carlo Rossi, the palace stands on a low stone terrace enclosed by openwork cast-iron railings. Its main colonnaded façade with ramps and a broad staircase faces the park, the opposite façade with a six-column semirotunda in the centre overlooks the Sredniaya Nevka. The staircase is ornamented with marble vases alternating with cast-iron flower-baskets. The interior decoration of the state rooms was executed by Stepan Pimenov, Vasily Demuth-Malinovsky, Giovanni Battista Scotti, Antonio Vighi, and others.

The palace was severely damaged by fire during the War of 1941–45. Its interiors have been restored by Mikhail Plotnikov in strict accordance with the original Rossi design. Often held in the palace are exhibitions of applied art, especially of artistic glass.

302 Kirovskaya Square

The compositional pivot of the square is the restrained and simple statue of Sergei Kirov, Soviet politician, which blends so well with the surrounding buildings. Erected in 1938, it ranks among the most outstanding achievements of Soviet monumental sculpture.

A particularly striking impression is produced by the building of the Kirovsky District Soviet, erected in 1931–34 by N. Trotsky. The asymmetric yet very expressive structure is situated along the axis of the Narva Triumphal Arch, slightly at an angle to Prospekt Stachek. The horizontality of the building is stressed by three rows of solid glassing. The building is flanked with a fifty-metre-high tower in the west. The tower lends a dynamic quality to the whole ensemble. There is a public garden laid out in the triangular-shaped square.

303 Statue of Kirov on Kirovskaya Square

The monument was designed by N. Tomsky and N. Trotsky and erected in front of the building of the Kirovsky District Soviet. It was unveiled on December 6, 1938. The monument is 15.5 metres high, the figure of Kirov, 7.7 metres high.

The pedestal is made of polished dark-green granite and adorned with bas-reliefs representing scenes from the Civil War and peaceful labour of the Soviet people. V. Isayeva, Ye. Turandin, and R. Taurit also took part in the work under the supervision of Tomsky.

304 Statue of Lenin on Moskovskaya Square

The authors of the monument, which was erected to mark the centenary of Lenin's birth, are Mikhail Anikushin and Valentin Kamensky. The monument fits well into its surroundings and forms the pivot of the square.

The great leader is presented as a tribune, his figure in motion as if he were addressing the people.

On the square behind the monument is the building of the House of Soviets erected in 1936–41 and designed by a team of architects under Noah Trotsky (Lev Tverskoi, Yakov Svirsky, Yakov Lukin, and others). The frieze was executed by Nikolai Tomsky, the State Emblem surmounting the frieze, by Igor Krestovsky.

305 The Moscow Triumphal Arch

A monument to the victories of Russian arms, the arch was erected in 1838 by Vasily Stasov at the entry into the city from the direction of Moscow. As cast-iron structures go, it is one of the largest of its kind: twelve mighty Doric columns support an entablature with eight trophies and a frieze decorated with thirty high-relief figures of winged genii. The figures of the genii and the trophies were modelled by Boris Orlovsky and cast by P. Zaburdin.

The arch was cast at the Alexandrovsky Iron Foundry under Vasily Stasov's supervision and restored in 1959–61 by Yevgenia Petrova.

306 The Moskovsky Victory Park

The Moskovsky Victory Park was laid out to commemorate the great victory of the Soviet people over Nazi Germany. Designed by Ye. Katonin and V. Kirkhoglani, it was started on October 7, 1945, and completed on July 7, 1946.

The park is a fortunate fusion of the formal and landscape styles. The Avenue of Heroes—the central walk—starts from the main entrance flanked with propylaea. The propylaea are adorned with bas-reliefs inspired by the Victory of 1945. Ranged along the avenue, on right and left, are the busts of Leningraders who were awarded the title of Hero of the Soviet Union two times in succession: Vasily Osipov, Victor Golubev, Yevgeny Fiodorov, Vasily Rakov, Semion Bogdanov, and Nikolai Chelnokov. A statue of Zoya Kosmodemyanskaya, Heroine of the Soviet Union, by M. Manizer, was put up in the park in 1951.

308 The Pulkovo Airport

The building was designed by A. Zhuk, G. Vlanin, V. Maximov, and others and erected in 1973. It is a flat prismatic structure topped by five frustum-shaped glazed towers. The latter are visible a great way off and are an organic part of the port's silhouette. The main hall whose roof rests on five mushroom-shaped supports opens on two sides—the main square and the airfield. It receives daylight not only through the windows but through ceiling lanterns as well.

309 Chernyshevsky Square. Monument to Chernyshevsky. Hotel Rossia (Russia)

Chernyshevsky Square adjoins one of the central Leningrad thoroughfares, Moskovsky Prospekt, laid out after the October Revolution. The authors of the monument to Nikolai Chernyshevsky, the Russian revolutionary democrat, which stands in the centre of the square, are V. Lishev and V. Yakovlev. A new hotel—Rossia—was built on the square after the War of 1941–45, and its façade provides an impressive background for the monument.

310 Hotel Pulkovskaya

This modern hotel building is a remarkable example of new Leningrad architecture. It is integrated in the ensemble of Victory Square, standing at the entrance to the city from the side of the Pulkovo Airport. The hotel was built by S. Speransky (head of the project) and V. Volonsevich (USSR), and Ilmo Valjaka and Olle Arviainen (Finland) between 1982 and 1984.
The austerity of its composition is emphasized by the use of white stone set off by dark decorative elements and bronze.

311 The former Cesme Church

Built in 1777–80 by Yury Velten, this is one of the few pseudo-Gothic structures in Leningrad architecture. The décor of the façades is based on an arbitrary treatment of Gothic motifs. The walls, ornamented with narrow vertical ribs and moulded pointed arches, are transpierced by tall lancet windows. The walls terminate in a low parapet with small, typically Gothic pinnacles. The church is quadrifoliate in plan: three rounded apses and a rounded narthex are attached to the main volume. Their vaults have partially retained their pseudo-Gothic moulded décor. The churchyard used to serve as the last resting-place for veterans of the Russian Army. Buried here during the War of 1941–45 were Soviet soldiers who fell in the defence of Leningrad.
The church building was restored in 1965–68.

312 The Lenin City Auditorium and Sports Hall

This is the city's largest covered stadium seating 25,000. It was opened in 1980, before the Moscow Olympic Games.

It was designed by a group of architects under N. Baranov and I. Chaiko and built under the supervision of A. Morozov, Yu. Yeliseyev and O. Kurbatov.
The building can be used for holding competitions in fourteen different sports, as well as for public meetings, festivals and concerts. It has the form of a huge cylinder; the diameter of its arena is 160 metres. The roofing is constructed like a gigantic membrane of steel cables and solid sheets, without any inner supports.
The laconic composition and decor harmonize with the purpose of the structure. The rhythm of the tall bearing columns of the façade is accentuated by the window openings.

314–318 Memorial to the Heroic Defenders of Leningrad

This monument commemorating the defenders of Leningrad who saved their city from enemy occupation in the War of 1941–45 is the work of Mikhail Anikushin, Sergei Speransky, and Valentin Kamensky. The majestic architectural and sculptural ensemble was erected near the former front line. Today, this is a residential area, with twenty-two-storey buildings flanking the highway. The memorial has become the centre of this new district, enriching its architectural aspect. There are elements in it of both the documentary and the symbolic. A ring of granite symbolizes the blockade of Leningrad. It rests on imperceptible supports and seems to hover in the air. In the centre of the open area, forty metres in diameter, formed by the ring, is a bronze sculptural group entitled *Blockade*, a striking composition with more than one meaningful message. The intrinsic dramatism of the scenes represented allowed the sculptor to dwell on the noble character of man, on his energy, resoluteness, and powers of resistance. It is in the image of the Mother that these feelings are most forcefully expressed, an image wherein is concentrated, as it were, the anguish and the wrath of all women who mourn the loss of their children.
Placed on pylons built of dark-red granite and flanking the wide flights of steps are sculptural groups that must inevitably command the attention of the viewer—*Soldiers*, *Sailors*, *Building the Defences*, *Casters*, and *People's Volunteers*. Near the obelisk is the focal group—*The Worker* and *The Soldier*. Together they form the impressive composition called *The Victors*. The postures and faces of the figures are the very incarnation of resolution and unconquerability. They personify not only the heroic people of Leningrad but also the victorious Soviet people as a whole.
The conceptual centre of the complex is a fifty-metre-high obelisk.
The memorial was inaugurated on May 9, 1975, the 30th anniversary of the victory over Nazi Germany.

319–321 The Green Belt of Glory

This is a memorial dedicated to the heroic defence of Leningrad during the War of 1941–45. It was created on the initiative of Mikhail Dudin, a Leningrad poet. The memorial is made up of various war relics—tanks, guns, and trucks raised from the bottom of Lake Ladoga. They were placed on pedestals and installed along the former front line. The total length of the memorial "belt" is 220 kilometres.

320 Memorial Milestone on the Road of Life

This memorial post designed by M. Meisel was erected on the shore of Lake Ladoga. 45 similar milestones mark every kilometre on the Road of Life between Leningrad and Lake Ladoga. This was the name given to the route, one hundred kilometres long, which during the siege of Leningrad linked the city with the Osinovets Cape on Lake Ladoga, and when the lake was frozen, with the small village of Kobon on the eastern shore of the lake. The uninterrupted activity of this legendary route was maintained at the cost of the lives of numerous drivers, sappers, railwaymen, soldiers, pilots, anti-aircraft gunners, and artillery men. It helped to supply the besieged city with food and munitions and to evacuate the starving Leningraders—children, women, and elderly people—to the "mainland".

321 The Broken Ring Memorial near Lake Ladoga

The monument was executed by K. Simun, V. Filippov, P. Melnikov, and I. Rybin.
It was put up by residents of the Kalininsky district of Leningrad between kilometres 39 and 40 of the Road of Life, at the Vaganovo decline to Lake Ladoga, where the legendary route across the ice began. The gap in the arch symbolizes the only outlet from the besieged city. The memorial was unveiled in January 1968.

322–329 The Piskariovskoye Memorial Cemetery

The memorial designed by Alexander Vasilyev and Yevgeny Levinson commemorates the courage and fortitude displayed by the people of Leningrad in the War of 1941–45. The bronze figure epitomizing the Motherland was modelled by Vera Isayeva and Robert Taurit (who also jointly executed the high-relief figures on the butt-ends of the side stelae).
Two pavilions with solemn and laconic inscriptions by Mikhail Dudin on their walls house an exhibition devoted to the heroic 900-day defence of Leningrad. They serve as propylaea that form the entrance into the necropolis. In the centre of a granite square enframed by a parapet is a bowl with the Flame of Remembrance. From here a flight of stairs leads to the mass graves and the statue of the Motherland. Behind the statue and on both sides of it are massive stelae of grey granite. Carved in the central stela are the words of a solemn epitaph by Olga Bergholz. The epitaph is flanked with high reliefs, three on each side, on themes from the life and defence of the besieged city. They were executed by M. Weinman, B. Kapliansky, A. Malakhin, and M. Kharlamova.
The memorial was inaugurated on May 9, 1960.
Buried here are about half a million persons who perished in the siege of Leningrad.

332 Ploshchad Muzhestva Metro Station

A new construction technique was worked out during the planning of the northern part of the Kirovsko-Vyborgskaya metro line which began to function in 1974–75. For the first time in the practice of constructing the underground, a single vault was used over the two railway lines with a platform between them. This technical principle was employed in two stations, Ploshchad Muzhestva and Politekhnicheskaya. The span of the vault is more than 18 metres. This novel construction lends these stations a special expressive quality. They are notable for their graceful proportions and architectural integrity. Both stations were designed by L. Shreter and S. Speransky.

334 Theatre for Young People

The new building of the theatre was erected in 1962 to mark the 40th anniversary of the foundation of the young pioneers' organization. The work was supervised by A. Zhuk. The building is noteworthy for its compositional clarity and simplicity. The façade overlooking Pionerskaya Square is decorated with mosaic panels by A. Mylnikov, A. Koroliov, and L. Kholina.

In front of the theatre, on Pionerskaya Square, is a statue of Alexander Griboyedov, Russian poet and statesman, designed by V. Lishev and V. Yakovlev.

345 The House of Flowers

In addition to the exhibition halls and a "Flowers from Bulgaria" shop this house incorporates a café. It was built on Kirovsky Prospekt, Petrogradskaya Side, in 1982 to the design of Zh. Verzhbitsky, I. Zhuravliova, and V. Meshcherin. Among those responsible for its interior decoration were the painters G. Shilo, A. Skriagin, and L. Lanets.

348, 349 Hotel Pribaltiyskaya

This seventeen-floor block of very imposing character was built in 1979 by the architects N. Baranov, S. Yevdokimov, V. Kovaliova, and the engineer P. Panfilov. The first building erected on the Gulf of Finland shore of Vasilyevsky Island, it was intended to be the dominant structure of the future seafront district.

351 Port Arrival and Departure building

In accordance with the general plan of Leningrad the "sea gates" to the city are being built on the western shore of Vasilyevsky Island.

The port building was designed by a group of architects under the supervision of V. Sokhin and constructed in 1982 by A. Nelipa and A. Fedorovich.

The walls of the building are faced with relief-work panels which look like sails filled out with wind. It is topped by a tower with a 74-metre spire.

354–382 Petrodvorets

The Great and Monplaisir Palaces are part of the Lower Park ensemble of Petrodvorets (formerly Peterhof), a magnificent monument of Russian architecture and landscape gardening in the 18th and first quarter of the 19th century.

The Great Palace, situated as it is on a high natural mound, presents a beautiful picture from the park and the sea. The construction of the palace was ordered by Peter the Great in January 1715. The first structure was a two-storey building which soon proved too small for court purposes and was rebuilt in 1745–55 by Bartolommeo Rastrelli.

Among those who worked on the improvement and enlargement of the palace in the second half of the 18th and the first decades of the 19th century were Yury Velten, who designed the White Banquet Hall, the Throne and Cesme Rooms; Jean-Baptiste Vallin de la Mothe, who was responsible for the interior decoration of the Chinese Lobbies; and Vasily Stasov.

In Soviet time, all the royal palaces were converted into museums and all the parks into rest and recreation areas for the working people. The first group of visitors, over 500 persons in all, entered the halls of the Great Palace as early as May 18, 1918.

During the War of 1941–45 the Nazi invaders reduced the Great Palace to a heap of rubble and inflicted enormous damage to most of the other structures of Petrodvorets. Restoration work on the palace was begun as soon as the town was liberated. The first to be re-opened was the Picture Room (originally designed by Rastrelli). This room is adorned with intricate gilt carving, its walls hung with three hundred and sixty-eight portraits by Pietro Rotari. The other interiors at present open to visitors are Peter the Great's Study with a décor restored to its original early 18th-century aspect, the Crown, Divan and Partridge Rooms (by Rastrelli), the White Banquet Hall, the Throne and Cesme Rooms (by Velten), and others. Complementary to the architectural décor of the interiors are works of figurative and applied art by outstanding Russian and Western European artists and craftsmen.

The Palace of Monplaisir was erected in 1714–24 by Johann Braunstein and Jean-Baptiste Le Blond. Its significance as an architectural monument is indeed inestimable: it is a structure typical of Russian suburban palaces of the early 18th century, which so singularly combined the new with the traditional in their architecture. The northern façade of the Monplaisir fronts the sea, and the building blends beautifully with the surrounding landscape. Its interiors are lavishly decorated with ceiling painting, stuccowork, lacquered panels, tiles, and gilding.

The Monplaisir ensemble is by now totally restored. Open to visitors are its Central Hall, Secretary's and Lacquer Rooms, Bedroom, Pantry, and two galleries. Hanging in the galleries is the collection of pictures that was evacuated in 1941. It was amassed by Peter the Great in the course of his trips abroad. Also on display are items of furniture, porcelain, and other works of art typical for palace interiors in the Petrine epoch.

The Lower Park and Upper Gardens are superb examples of the formal type of park. The pivot of the park ensemble is the Great Palace. Its southern façade overlooks the Upper Gardens whose lay-out is organically linked with the compositional scheme of the palace. A large green parterre before the palace allows the latter to be viewed from the very entrance to the park. Situated along the palace's central axis are the Neptune and Oak fountains, and just in front of the palace, in large square pools, are the Spring and Summer fountains. Construction of the Lower Park on the shore of the Gulf of Finland was begun in 1710 on the order of Peter the Great, who also suggested its general lay-out. The task was accomplished by the architects Jean-Baptiste Le Blond, Mikhail Zemtsov, Niccolo Michetti, Johann Braunstein, master gardeners Leonardt van Harnigfeld, and Anton Borisov. The park produces an impression of solemn grandeur with its numerous fountains, the gilt and marble statuary, and the splendour of the Great Palace on its grounds. The natural mound on which the palace stands is adorned with terraces, two monumental staircases, and the Great Cascade which is linked to the Sea Canal. The sea lends the park an enchantment all its own. Because of its nearness the fountains seem fashioned by nature itself. In all, the Lower Park is graced by a hundred and forty-two fountains and three cascades.

Outstanding among these fountains is the Great Cascade completed in 1800–4 by Andrei Voronikhin, who put up two colonnades on each side of the cascade.

The centrepiece of the Great Cascade, Samson Rending Open the Jaws of a Lion, symbolizes the battle of Poltava in 1709, the decisive encounter of the Great Northern War. Stolen by the Nazis during their occupation of the town, the sculpture of the cascade was recreated by the Soviet sculptors Vasily Simonov (the Samson group), Igor Krestovsky, Nikolai Dydykin, Vadim Sokolov, and others.

The Petrodvorets water-supply system, built in the early 18th century by the hydraulic engineer Vasily Tuvolkov, the architects Mikhail Zemtsov and I. Ustinov, is unique: unlike the fountains of European parks which were fed by machinery, utilized here is the natural decline of the terrain from the Ropsha Heights (22 kilometres from Petrodvorets) to the sea. Ground waters gather into fourteen reservoirs by way of canals, then flow to the fountains through pipes. Amassed at the top of the slope, the water, when released, rushes down the pipes with great force and erupts to the surface through the fountain nozzles in sparkling jets of spray. The pressure of the water is so strong that the jet of Samson, the park's main fountain, shoots up to a height of 22 metres.

Aside from the fountains and cascades the Lower Park is notable for several architectural pieces, among them the Hermitage Pavilion and the Marly Palace, both designed by Johann Braunstein and put up in the 1720s.

The most important feature of the third Petrodvorets park, Alexandria, is the Cottage Pavilion built by Adam Menelaws in 1829. The pointed pediments and lancet arches show the influence of the Gothic style. The terraces and balconies add to its modest but refined décor. The interiors were designed by Giovanni Battista Scotti who worked in Russia in the first half of the 19th century.

383–398 Town of Lomonosov

The Upper Park ensemble of the town of Lomonosov (formerly Oranienbaum) consists of the Chinese Palace, the Palace of Peter III and the Coasting Hill Pavilion. Up to 1917 the palaces of Oranienbaum served as the summer residences of the royal family and aristocracy. After the October Revolution they were declared the property of the people. The parks were turned into recreation areas, the palaces into museums.

The Chinese Palace was designed by Antonio Rinaldi and built in 1762–68. Rinaldi's project was implemented by talented folk craftsmen—moulders, marblers, mosaicists, wood-carvers. The most interesting interiors are the Hall of the Muses and the Grand Hall. The Lilac Drawing-room, the Buglework and Gold Rooms are especially striking for the rich variety of their décor. The palace's ceilings were painted by well-known Italian masters of the Venetian academic school.

The name, Chinese Palace, stems from the chinoiserie décor in four of its rooms. The palace's unique parquetry which was executed after Rinaldi's drawings by Russian craftsmen has survived to our day.

The Palace of Peter III was built in 1756–62 by Rinaldi. The rooms of the top floor are richly decorated. Especially interesting are the stuccowork ornamentation of the ceilings and the lacquered panels of the doors. The unique collection of porcelain, furniture, wood-, stone- and bone-carvings, embroidery, and painted enamels is also an integral part of the décor.

The Coasting Hill Pavilion was erected in 1762–74 by Rinaldi. Originally there was a sloping roadway running down from the pavilion along which special cars took people for amusement rides. In the 19th century, the roadway fell into decay and was dismantled. The lithe, slender silhouette of the building blends harmoniously with the surrounding landscape. Radiant and beautiful are the pavilion's interiors—the Circular Hall, the Porcelain and Hunters' Rooms with their ornamental painting, stuccowork and wood-carving.

399–424 Town of Pushkin

The Catherine Palace, a remarkable monument of Russian 18th-century culture, is the compositional centre of the architectural and park ensemble of the town of Pushkin (formerly Tsarskoye Selo). Among those who took part in its creation were the Russian architects Alexei Kvasov and Sabbas Chevakinsky, as well as numerous artists, sculptors, and craftsmen. The palace was completed by Bartolommeo Rastrelli in 1752–56. Its façade, which is over 300 metres long, has a rich and varied décor. Its many columns, pilasters, sculptured figures, the openwork railings of its balconies, and the vivid colours of its walls lend an air of sublime elegance and festivity to the structure. The palace's state rooms adorned with gilt wood-carving constitute the Golden Suite, one of Rastrelli's most beautiful creations. In the 1780s, some of Rastrelli's interiors were redecorated by Charles Cameron in the Classical style. After the fire of 1820 Vasily Stasov was called in to remedy the damage caused to the Catherine Palace. He restored Rastrelli's and Cameron's interiors and created some new ones. Following the October Revolution the palaces and parks of Tsarskoye Selo were taken over by the state. The Catherine Palace became a museum of art and history, the parks were turned into areas of rest and recreation for the public. In 1937, the town was renamed Pushkin in honour of the great Russian poet, who spent his school years (1811–17) at the Lyceum in Tsarskoye Selo.

With the outbreak of war in 1941 the Soviet Government ordered the museum's collections evacuated inland. The town was captured by the enemy in September 1941. The Nazi soldiers ransacked the palace, and before retreating in January 1944 set it on fire. German troops also caused heavy damage to the parks: the pavilions and bridges were destroyed, the trees wantonly cut down.

Soviet restorers have brought the Catherine Palace back to life: sixteen interiors are now open to viewers.

Among these are the Main Staircase (by Bartolommeo Rastrelli), the Great Hall (by Hippolyte Monighetti), the Picture Hall (by Bartolommeo Rastrelli), the Green Dining-room, the Blue Room, the Painting Lobby (by Charles Cameron), and others.

The parks of Pushkin rank among the finest creations of Russian landscape gardening. They were laid out by Sabbas Chevakinsky, Bartolommeo Rastrelli, Vasily Neyelov, Yury Velten, Charles Cameron and Adam Menelaws, the landscape gardeners Jan Roosen, Joseph Busch, and T. Ilyin at about the time the Catherine Palace was being built. Tens of thousands of serfs took part in their construction.

In 1780–94, Cameron erected an outstanding classical ensemble on the Catherine Palace's grounds: the Cold Baths with the Agate Rooms, the Promenade Gallery (now called the Cameron Gallery), the Hanging Garden, and a gently sloping ramp.

In 1900, a monument to Pushkin by Roman Bach was unveiled in the Lyceum Garden. In the Catherine Park memories of Pushkin are evoked by the Lyceists' Walk and the sculpture *Girl with a Pitcher* by Pavel Sokolov, to which the poet dedicated one of his lyrics.

The Catherine Palace was fronted by the formal part of the park, which had a geometrically precise lay-out. In the late 18th century this area began to undergo a gradual transformation, losing much of its original aspect. After the War of 1941–45 it was decided to restore the formal section from 18th-century drawings.

The park stands out for its straight avenues flanked with mighty century-old trees, green plots, and white marble statuary, the mirror-smooth waters of Big Lake with its green banks and shoreline architecture—the Hermitage and the Grotto (by Bartolommeo Rastrelli), the Admiralty and Marble Bridge (by Vasily Neyelov). In the 1770s, memorials were erected on its grounds dedicated to the victories in the Russo-Turkish war of 1768–74: the Orlov Gate and the Cesme Column by Antonio Rinaldi, the Kagul Obelisk by Yury Velten, and others.

The Alexander Park is one of the largest landscape parks in the country, though the part that borders on the Catherine Park has to a certain degree retained its regular lay-out. Shady walks, wide sunlit lawns, small pools and canals spanned by elegant bridges lend it an inimitable charm.

425–445 Pavlovsk

The Pavlovsk Palace is an architectural monument of the late 18th and first quarter of the 19th century brought into being by the joint efforts of outstanding architects and sculptors.

The palace's design, typical of the suburban mansions of the period, was by Charles Cameron, who put up the central block in 1782–86. In 1796–99, Vincenzo Brenna enlarged the complex by adding two symmetrically disposed service blocks and a palace church. He also created some new interiors: the Picture Gallery, the Throne Room, and others.

In 1803, the central block was damaged by fire. The restoration of the interiors was entrusted to Andrei

Voronikhin who elaborated and partially altered their décor. Together with Giacomo Quarenghi, Voronikhin was responsible for the lay-out and decoration of the rooms on the ground floor.

The last in the line of talented architects who worked in Pavlovsk was Carlo Rossi. He designed the Corner Drawing-room in 1816 and the Palace Library in 1822–24.

The combined efforts of all these architects plus those of the sculptors (Ivan Prokofyev, Ivan Martos, Mikhail Kozlovsky, Vasily Demuth-Malinovsky) and the artists (Giovanni Battista Scotti, Johann Mettenleiter, Andrei Martynov, and Pietro Gonzaga) brought into being a complete, integrated architectural complex. Notwithstanding the participation of so many artists in the construction and decoration of the palace, it demonstrates an amazing stylistic unity illustrating the evolution of Classicism in Russian architecture in the late 18th and first quarter of the 19th century.

The Soviet government went to great pains to preserve Pavlovsk in the stormy days of the October Revolution and the grim, gruelling years of the Civil War. In 1918, a museum of history and art was organized on the palace premises.

During the War of 1941–45 Pavlovsk was occupied by Nazi troops. Before retreating they burnt the palace down. Today, all of its forty-five interiors have been completely restored. Among these are such masterpieces of Classical architecture as the Italian and Grecian Halls, the Dressing-room, the Dining-room (by Cameron and Brenna), the Upper Vestibule, the Halls of War and of Peace, the Grand Hall, the Picture Gallery, the Church Gallery (by Brenna), the Pilaster Room (by Quarenghi), the Little Lantern (by Voronikhin), and the Rossi Library.

The museum has on display unique works of art. The collection of antique sculpture housed in the palace ranks among the richest in the country, second only to that of the Hermitage. The picture gallery boasts many canvases by well-known Western European artists of the 17th and 18th centuries. There is also a superb collection of tapestries and *objets d'art* in bronze, ivory, and valuable minerals.

The Pavlovsk Park (600 hectares) was created by the famous Russian architects of the late 18th and early 19th century, in the course of fifty years, beginning from 1777. It is one of the most beautiful landscape parks in the world.

Many of the park's pavilions put up in the 1780s and '90s were designed by Cameron, among them the Temple to Friendship, the Apollo Colonnade, the Aviary, the Pavilion of the Three Graces, and others.

Erected in the early 19th century were Visconti and Peel-Tower Bridges designed by Voronikhin, Cast-iron Bridge and the Rossi Pavilion by Rossi, and Paul's Mausoleum by Thomas de Thomon.

In spite of its having been created over a period of fifty years by a succession of architects, the park is compositionally an integral ensemble, its constituent elements fused together by an original artistic concept.

Photographs by: ALEXEI ANANCHENKO—137; SERGEI ALEXEYEV and VALENTIN BARANOVSKY—fore-title, 16, 17, 19, 52, 53, 186, 192, 194, 199, 201, 207, 208, 209, 210, 241, 251, 260, 265, 268, 274, 346; VALENTIN BARANOVSKY—1, 12, 14, 27, 29, 48, 231, 317; VALERY BARNEV—78, 131, 383, 388, 393, 396, 411, 414, 417; YURI BELINSKY—221; LEONID BOGDANOV—71, 121, 122; MOISEI BYTKA—28, 60, 72, 239, 243, 287, 293, 297, 298, 299, 310, 311, 316, 331, 333, 340, 343, 344, 345, 347, 351; MOISEI BYTKA and KIRA ZHARINOVA—248; NIKOLAI CHAPLIN—136, 235; BORIS CHEREMISIN—219, 242, 353; VLADIMIR DAVYDOV—421, 445; PAVEL DEMIDOV and OLEG TRUBSKY—3, 10, 25, 38, 40, 43, 54, 58, 59, 73, 75, 76, 85, 188, 218, 227, 230, 277, 288, 289, 295, 301, 309, 349, 352; NATALYA and KONSTANTIN DOKA—24, 324, 325, 326, 327, 366, 368, 370, 371, 372, 373, 378, 381, 392; VLADIMIR DOROKHOV—425, 426, 438; VLADIMIR FABRITSKY and IGOR SHMELIOV—6, 47, 65, 66, 70, 154, 237, 337, 410; SERGEI FALIN—23, 30, 31, 32, 33, 35, 39, 45, 51, 80, 83, 125, 126, 128, 130, 132, 134, 141, 142, 144, 145, 147, 148, 149, 150, 153, 155, 156, 161, 183, 184, 203, 211, 216, 217, 220, 223, 229, 249, 250, 254, 255, 276, 284, 285, 286, 294, 322, 335, 348, 412, 418, 432; GRIGORY KHATIN—272, 273, 399, 402, 403; ROMUALD KIRILLOV—270, 296, 404; ROMUALD KIRILLOV and EVGENY MONTLEVICH—13, 308; FERDINAND KUZIUMOV—159, 292; BORIS KUZMIN—283, 436; BORIS KUZNETSOV—279; BORIS MANUSHIN—332; RAFAIL MAZELEV—200; VLADIMIR MELNIKOV—36, 61, 135, 143, 146, 151, 185, 213, 225, 226, 228, 314, 360, 367, 376, 409, 413, 420, 435; MIKHAIL MIKISHATYEV—206, 246; EVGENY MONTLEVICH—62, 152, 189, 266, 271, 408; EVGENY PLIUKHIN—157, 158; OLEG POLESHCHUK—15, 20, 196, 202, 204, 205, 234, 247, 253, 321; VLADIMIR SAMOILOV—2, 21, 41, 44, 74, 81, 127, 162, 193, 215, 236, 280, 304, 305, 312, 313, 315, 329, 338, 339, 341, 342, 350, 354; VICTOR SAVIK—86, 87, 88, 89, 90, 91, 129, 198, 282; GRIGORY SHABLOVSKY—34, 240, 330; NIKOLAI SHALIAKIN—232, 233; VLADIMIR SHLAKAN—56, 385, 387, 390, 391, 395; BORIS SMELOV—57, 244, 384, 394, 397; VLADIMIR SOBOLEV and KIRA ZHARINOVA—5, 7, 8, 9, 11, 18, 26, 46, 49, 67, 68, 84, 190, 214, 222, 245, 261, 264, 267, 278, 290, 291, 318, 336, 355, 356, 365, 369, 374, 375, 401, 407, 429, 434, 440, 441, 442, 443, 444; VLADIMIR STREKALOV—4, 22, 42, 50, 55, 63, 64, 77, 79, 82, 163, 166, 181, 197, 212, 252, 256, 257, 258, 259, 300, 302, 303, 334; BORIS STUKALOV—182; VLADIMIR STUKALOV—139, 140, 187, 262, 269; LEONID TARAZEVICH—359, 361, 362, 363, 364, 379, 380; DAVID TRAKHTENBERG—191; MIKHAIL VELICHKO—357, 358, 377, 382, 386, 389, 398, 419, 422, 423, 424, 427, 428, 430, 431; IGOR YASEVICH—195; LEONID ZIVERT—133, 138, 160, 164, 224, 263, 306, 328, 400, 405, 406, 415, 416.

ЛЕНИНГРАД. ИСКУССТВО И АРХИТЕКТУРА

Альбом (на английском языке)

Издание второе

Издательство «Аврора». Ленинград. 1990

Изд. № 2461. (26-70)

Пленки для цветной печати изготовлены
в Первой Образцовой типографии, Москва

Printed and bound in Austria by Globus, Vienna